Screwed

Five Plays

Stephen Goldberg

Fomite
Burlington, VT

Copyright 2013 © by Stephen Goldberg

All rights reserved. No part of this book may be reproduced in any form or by any means without the prior written consent of the publisher, except in the case of brief quotations used in reviews and certain other noncommercial uses permitted by copyright law.

This is a work of fiction. Names, characters, places and incidents are either the product of the author's imagination or are used fictitiously. Any resemblance to actual persons, living or dead, events or locales is entirely coincidental.

ISBN-13: 978-1-937677-52-7
Library of Congress Control Number: 2013945951

Fomite
58 Peru Street
Burlington, VT 05401
www.fomitepress.com

Cover Design - Paul Schnabel
Front cover photo - Inger Dybfest
Back cover photo - Joseph Goldberg

Screwed

Five Plays

The Plays of Stephen J. Goldberg

Waiting for Angels 2013
Who's Afraid of Edward Albee 2010
Hell is a Goddess 2009
The Third Rail 2009
Flying on the Bright Wings of Despair 2005
Sluts on the Roof 2004
Hollywood 2003
Don and Tom 2003
Rough Landing on a Soft Cranium 2002
Kong Wash 2001
Arnie Gets it Good 2000
One Mistake 1999
Burning Bridges 1999
End Zone 1998
The Delivery 1998
Screwed 1997
Ballroom of Forgiveness 1997
Curbdivers of Redemption 1997
Taboo of Fantasy 1996
Interior Demolition with a Brando Obsession 1995
Quantum Dog in a Deep Blue Jaguar 1995
The Truth Has No Heart 1993
Sunspot; The Crime of the Need to be Right 1985
Sand Trap 1982

More information
Curbdiver@aol.com

Contents

Screwed	1
Arnie Gets It Good	65
Kong Wash	111
Curbdivers of Redemption	177
Don and Tom	259

Acknowledgments

First and foremost my late wife, singer/songwriter/actress, Rachel Bissex, who never stopped believing in me.
Paul Schnabel, brilliant actor and friend who made my plays come alive.
Jay Goldberg , my dear brother, who taught me to follow the muse.
My parents, Edna and Joseph Goldberg who put me through hell to make me strong.
My wonderful children: Emma, Jonas, Matt.
Bobby Fracter, my teenage junkie guru.
The Fomite Press for making this book something real.
A bit of thanks to vodka, for its danger and comfort.
Thanks for my sailboat on the lake, that makes life a dream.
Thanks for the wind, the sky and the unknowable.

Introduction

These plays were written with the feeling of jazz, which has been my life long profession and love.

Not that the music in them is jazz, but with a feeling of spontaneity, which is the way they should be performed. With the feel of improvisation.

Minimal sets, cubes of different sizes that can be moved by the actors in scene changes.
Making much use of creative lighting and sound design.

My plays have no heroes — meaning that all the characters are victims, virgins to the lines they speak. The feeling that they have never been said before and will never be said again.

Blocking should be simple, we don't want to wear out the floor.

I do write about the Underbelly of Humanity. Growing up in New York City has left its forever mark on me. The beautiful, sometimes brilliant, sometimes dangerous, anti-heroes have given me their forgotten gifts.

These plays are my payback to them, who unknowingly gave me so much, with their beauty, humor and danger.

Most, or all of them are gone, the "house wreckers and mind fuckers" as we called them on the lower east side of New York.

I dedicate these plays to them.

Stephen Goldberg

SCREWED

Screwed 1997

First Production, Off Center for the Dramatic Arts
Burlington, VT
Directed by the Author

Original Cast
Artie – Paul Soychak
Leo – Paul Schnabel
Tess – Tracey Girdich
Lori – Aimee Loiselle

Cast of Characters

LEO – A psychotic man, under house arrest
ARTIE – A strange garbage picker
TESS – A woman from an escort service
LORI – A woman from an escort service

Screwed

As the house is opening, before any dialogue starts, LEO is trying to do mundane things, make a sandwich, sweep up, wash some dishes, maintenance kind of stuff, cleaning himself, trying just to function. A radio is on between stations.

(Kicking on door from outside.)

ARTIE

Open up, Leo.

LEO

Who is it?

ARTIE

For Christ sakes Leo, open the door.

LEO

Who is it?

ARTIE

It's me, now open up.

LEO

Artie?

ARTIE

Yeah.

LEO

Where's your key?

                           ARTIE
I can't get to it, okay, open the damn door, Leo.

                            LEO
Artie?

                           ARTIE
Open the damn door.

*LEO opens door. Enter ARTIE. ARTIE, with grocery bags and crap from the street and a **large metal monolith** type object, which is **a piece of a heating duct**, he's struggling to carry all the found stuff.*

                            LEO
Jesus, man.

                           ARTIE
Check it out Leo, look at this… I found all this on the street. Leo?

                            LEO
Yeah, yeah, so what…

                           ARTIE
It's useful, you see that don't you Leo?

                            LEO
Yeah, yeah, I see it.

                           ARTIE
You hungry, I got some bread and stuff.

                            LEO
Any butter?

                           ARTIE
No, no butter, but look at this thing…

LEO
You keep bringing crap in here, I can't find anything, there's too much crap. LOOK OUT!

ARTIE
What, what?

LEO
The things flying around, they're around your head. Artie, look out. There's no gravity in this place. This place is fucked.

ARTIE
So go out. Once in a while go out, get out of here.

LEO
I can't, okay, I can't, I'm workin on that, you know that.

ARTIE
You need some fresh air.

LEO
I'm workin on it, don't tell me what to do or what I need, I can't take that. I'm doin the best I can, okay, okay motherfucker?

ARTIE
Okay, I mean you're doin good, we're doin good. I just want you to get some color, you look good, you do man, you just need a little color that's all. You been in here for months.

LEO
House arrest, you ever hear of it. You think I wear this thing (*showing ankle bracelet*) to look cool, it doesn't come off Artie.

ARTIE
(*going through the stuff he's found*)
I'm just sayin you need some color.

LEO
What do I need color for, why don't you find a damn tanning bed, schlep that up here. The more crap the better. (*Seeing something fly by*) Holy shit!

ARTIE
Every time I give you a fuckin positive suggestion, you get all weird, I'm not tryin to hurt you, you know that. (*Pause*) You hungry?

LEO
I'm okay, I had some bacon, I made some bacon on the hot…(*Seeing things*) Oh man, Jesus, man.

ARTIE
Listen Leo, I got plans Leo, look at this, (*monolith*), it's a sign man, a spiritual symbol, a sign.

LEO
It's over, just look out, Artie, they're all over the place, it's over.

ARTIE
Over.

LEO
Yeah, all of it, they're gonna eat us alive, tonight, teeth and all, they can digest teeth and bones and fingernails, cartilage, they got power enzymes in their digestive systems, you understand that, you get that, power enzymes.

ARTIE
Yeah, well this thing is the anti-power-enzyme mother. Come on man, Leo, look at this, (*referring to monolith*) it's a transcendental sign. It has its own fuckin mathematical qualities. Touch it man. It'll burn your hand off, because you don't believe.

LEO
I don't believe, no way, no how. Everything's filled with terror. We're done for. It's a hollow piece of sheet metal bullshit, Look out man, they're gonna fly up your ass and down your throat and eat you alive!

ARTIE
Get off it…Leo listen, they'll fly inside this thing and get disintegrated, it'll zap them, they're attracted to it, like those bug zapper things, okay, so you're safe now.

LEO
I'm scared, Artie, I don't know what's happening.

ARTIE
You want me to hold you?

LEO
No! Don't!

ARTIE
What is it?

LEO
Everything, the phone book, the table, the window, the sounds, all of it, my mind, my own mind, the voices that won't stop talking about perfection, change this, fix that, be something, do some good in the world. These things man, things, flying around.

ARTIE
Look at this. (*Showing LEO some found silverware. ARTIE holds a setting of silverware hanging vertically from a string.*)

LEO
Jesus, wow man. (*Looking at silverware*)

ARTIE
Amazing isn't it.

LEO
What is this stuff…Oh man, the thing just missed me, oh man.

ARTIE
Did you take anything, any drugs, anything…

LEO
No nothing, nothing, Jesus, no, no, nothing, my own voice, Jesus… (*Silverware*) It's beautiful, like a shiny little family of stuff, (*studying silverware*) the same DNA, but like each one has its own function. The tops have this like same pattern, but the bottoms, all different. (*Pause*) Artie they're at us, they're killin' us, aren't they?

ARTIE
I'm telling you Leo this thing (*Monolith*) is gonna do its thing. What more can I do?

LEO
You?

ARTIE
Yeah me, what more Leo?

LEO
You.

ARTIE
Yeah me, you look bad, what is it, don't freak out on me, what is it Leo? Look, this thing (*Monolith*) has the signature of perfection. Leo, check it out.

LEO
I can't, I'm freaked, okay.

ARTIE
I'm sick of you being freaked. What Leo, what is it?

LEO
Everything, fuckin everything, I mean this family (*silverware*) everything about this is right… We're screwed man, you're like a miner who finds all this shit, it's worthless man, you're a gatherer, the shit has no worth, unsaleable. It's over, Artie, it's over, I want God to take me. Take me motherfucker! Here's my heart God, Hey man! (*Pause*) See there's no one there, no answer.

ARTIE
Leo, We've been through a lot of shit, you and me, I'll hold your hand, hold on man. He's in there, (*referring to monolith*) we're okay, hold my hand Leo.

LEO
I can't, I wish I could, it's bad and can only get worse.

ARTIE
You want to go to the hospital. Leo. You want to go back, is house arrest worse.

LEO
No! God no, not that please, please not that, not the... what... what did you say...what was it? (*Seeing things*)

ARTIE
Hospital, Leo, you didn't smoke any pot did you, you don't handle pot that well.

LEO
God no, not the... what, what was it? Artie!

ARTIE
Hospital, Leo, the hospital. I should take you back...

LEO
No, please no, not that, please no, my God, what is this crap? SHIT!

ARTIE
You're scaring me man, stop it, Leo stop it, you're scaring me.

LEO
I can't, I can't stop it, I can't, it's racing, my heart man, it's racing, Jesus I can't stand my voice. That thing, what is it man? (*Picking up broom, swinging it around*).

ARTIE

Don't hurt it man. Okay Leo, this is a monolith, it attracts the things, the bad things. Okay. It's a shield of protection.

LEO

You don't get it, do you? You're not my friend, you just want my SSI checks. You're the fuckin screw.

ARTIE

Come at me, with the broom, come at me. I'm a fucking super hero, come on Leo! Come on!

LEO

I'll smash you, my friend, I'll kill you. (*Smashing around a bit*) Artie, I have no strength, no power. I can't move. (*Drops broom*)

ARTIE

Take a nap man, get some rest, go to sleep.

LEO

No, no sleep, they'll get me if I sleep, don't tell me to sleep, you want them to get me don't you, don't you? You do, Jesus. That's when they get you, when you sleep.

ARTIE

Who, who'll get you, tell me... Leo... who? Be descriptive.

LEO

The things, the sky people, but they're not people, they're like birds and bats but with human faces. I don't know, somethin's wrong, bad, it is, isn't it, it's bad, it's bad, it's finally really bad. Artie, somethin is not there, missing. I wish the fuckin TV worked.

ARTIE

It's gone pal. No TV. No laugh tracks. Here, Leo, take some fuckin pills, you'll feel better.

LEO

No!

ARTIE
You'll feel better, they work, they're from the doctor.

LEO
No, he wants me to die, you want me to die, Jesus Christ, they're in the walls, look out, the walls and the floor, man oh man. It's all compressed Artie, I swear to God, it's compressed.

ARTIE
Leo you're scaring me, take the goddam pills, Leo look how pretty they are, multi-colored, things of beauty, you need some beauty in your life. You don't want to feel better, do you?

LEO
I don't need that crap, artificial crap. I miss my wife, I miss my driver's license, I miss my manhood, man. Come on fuckers, come on, you want to mess with me, come on, come on! That thing scares me, they're in there, you're telling me they're in there. I don't want this thing around my ankle. You are telling me, all the bad things are in that thing. All the surveillance cameras and shit.

ARTIE
Yeah man and they're gettin zapped. Look man, Leo. Listen, hear the little clicks.

LEO
Artie, over there, and over there, and Jesus…

ARTIE
What! Where, what are they, where, stop, stop it man.

LEO
They're bad, really bad, get away. You don't need me to hang out with, you deal, you deal with the outside, I'm gone man. Why do you hang out with me?

ARTIE
Please Leo, take the pills.

LEO
Give me the fuckin pills.

ARTIE
Here. Good. Take them. That's good Leo. Leo the lion.

LEO
The Lion.

ARTIE
Swallow babe. The Lion.

LEO
You're trying to kill me, you, it's you, they're gonna get you too, Jesus, I won't take them.

ARTIE
Fuck Leo, swallow. Look at it, it's a work of art, listen, Leo. (*Drumming on the monolith*) Is that cool, swallow man.

LEO
I can't man. I can't swallow without water.

ARTIE
Look. (*ARTIE swallows a few pills without water*) Boom, done.

LEO
Okay, I'm as good as you. (*He swallows*)

ARTIE
Good babe, you're gonna be okay, you're better than me. I promise, because you did this for me, when my mind was fucked. I'm stickin with you.

LEO
We're nothing, is that right, nothing, specks in the universe, bullshit, we're bullshit, right, is that right? Nothing.

ARTIE
Nothing, as far as the Milky Way is concerned, it doesn't give a fuck.

LEO

Not at all.

ARTIE

Not at all

LEO

Not at all, if I'm scared, the Milky Way doesn't give a shit. Right?

ARTIE

Right.

LEO

I'm scared man.

ARTIE

I know you are.

LEO

I'm seeing scary things, monsters and shit. I'm tryin to understand.

ARTIE

I know you are, I've been through it, and you took care of me, so I take care of you.

LEO

Fuck man! A thing flew over me, and over you, over all of us. (*Pause*) So that's a cool name, "The Milky Way". Artie who thought of that, that name, Milky Way. Milk man, so white, pure, who thought of it.

ARTIE

I thought of it! One clear night, I was up on the roof, scared, like you are now, no lights, a black out, the whole city, and the sky was so lit up, and this fuckin mass of dots of light, like a tit but better than a tit, but worse cause I couldn't touch it or suck it, the big mamma. I jerked off and wanted to come into the sky, shoot right into the universe, fuckin impregnate the sweet milky way, but the come, just went a few inches. Bad fuckin deal Leo, you know why.

LEO

Why. Artie, why?

ARTIE

Because, my dear friend, the sky can't be fucked.

LEO

I knew it, the sky can't be fucked. I fucking knew it, I told you, I knew it, they got us, they got me, I'm gone man, Artie, I'm gone, I'm out of here. If the sky can't be fucked, what can, I'm…I can't move, my God, I can't move, I need to run, I can't move, my legs don't work, my legs don't move. If you can't fuck the sky what's the point of living, there's no point.

ARTIE

The reason the sky can't be fucked is it's too far gone, in terms of light years… We are screwed Leo. Leo! Cool out, just cool out. Now I light this match, and you see it right off, now imagine if I lit it and you had to sit there for a year before it reached your eyes, that's a light year man. And these motherfuckers are talking millions and billions of light years. So the shit we see in the sky, the Milky Way, is not even there, so I'm jerking off and getting all excited about some shit that's not even there. If that's not stupid what is?

LEO

It's pretty stupid Artie.

ARTIE

You wish you could die, and not steal, and relapse into your criminal mind, and rape women in doorways and shoplift in fucking cheap department stores. You don't do that anymore, you don't go out. House arrest. Fight it, Leo. I'm here for you.

LEO

Artie, I'm paralyzed, they're all over me and I can't do anything about it. What does that make me? Nothing. A nothing with an ankle bracelet.

ARTIE

Leo!

LEO
What…

ARTIE
You want me to get some girls?

LEO
Some what!

ARTIE
Girls, women, ladies, babes, hot babes, slipping and sliding all over the place, some wet mouths to kiss us, some love girls?

LEO
Are you nuts, I'm paralyzed from the waist down, all over, I'm numb it's all over, no feeling.

ARTIE
Girls, Leo, beautiful girls. Bright lights reflected in beautiful innocent eyes. (*Goes at LEO*). Tenderness man.

LEO
Get… get… get off me, they're all over me.

ARTIE
Women Leo, we need women, affection, sex, lovemaking, conversation, contact with something real. Girls, man. (*LEO picks up chair*) If the nut house was just a big party scene, where people had fun and made love, and made jokes and the shrinks were more like Jackie Mason and Rodney Dangerfield, and Lenny Bruce and Fat Jackie Leonard, and we had great gourmet food and drank the best wine, and they gave us beautiful clothes and money, then we might get fucking well. But no, they just torture us more.

LEO
(*With chair*)
They're on you man, sucking your brains out. Keep away man, just step back, I'll kill you first, I will, before you get me.

ARTIE

I'm callin' an ambulance. Come on man, Leo, put down the chair.

LEO

The what, what did you call me?

ARTIE

The chair Leo, you want to smash my head in, is that it ? Here it is. Here's my head.

LEO

The chair, like a choir, I break your head, what's inside there.

ARTIE

Put it down. Leo. Put it down.

(*LEO puts the chair down*)

LEO

You don't know any girls, you don't know shit. I can't move.

ARTIE

You're on your feet Leo, you're a fighter, you think you're paralyzed, you're not, how far man, from your brain to your feet, we'll do the tape measure, (*ARTIE measures LEO with a tape measure*) you're okay… Okay Leo. Leo the chair man. The chairman.

LEO

Don't call me that. Get away from me. Get away. Girls, girls, you don't know any girls.

ARTIE

Ask the monolith pal, I know plenty of girls, and beautiful ones. You want one. Leo! You want a beautiful girl. I know you do. Sweet smelling. Soft talking, sweet girls, beautiful women.

LEO

(*Kneeling in front of monolith*)

Take me, take me, for I have sinned…I have done terrible things… I want to do more terrible things, forgive me, I have killed.

ARTIE
Leo! You want a girl? A girlfriend to take a walk with, to look in fucking store windows with, to look at menus with, and plan a fucking vacation with. To pick out a jacket with. Leo! To hug and kiss and fuckin buy soap with, you want that pal?

LEO
Yeah, yeah, sure, a girl. A girlfriend.

ARTIE
That-a-boy, you see, you see, you're okay, you have natural human desires, we'll get some beautiful girls over here and have a party, it's been years hasn't it…

LEO
Yeah, so what of it? I killed somebody, I did, I was put in a hospital for the criminally insane, that's bad man, it's bad, so the system watches my ankle, where I go what I do.

ARTIE
Leo! Stop scaring me, I don't mind when you steal from me, or play the radio too loud in between stations, or burn bacon on the hot plate, but don't go into this…

LEO
They're all over you. Like little replicas of the guy I killed. Oh my God… My God… I knew it.

ARTIE
You're giving me a heart attack, you son-of-a-bitch. You need affection, human contact, skin man, skin. A woman Leo, it could turn it all around, some love.

LEO
Okay, okay, get me a girl, get the beautiful girls, I don't see any girls. (*To monolith*) You're no girl, you're Christ, the Godhead. Artie, where'd you find him? I don't want him to watch us with the girls. In fuckin Egypt there was no watching, bastard, you get that?

ARTIE

Gimme the phone book.

LEO

Get it away from me, take it, take the son of a bitch thing. No! Don't go near it. What are you gonna do, Artie! What are you damn doing. Don't scare me. I tried to mug this old guy, old fucker in a gray overcoat. I killed him…don't touch the book. It's a death list, everyone in there will be dead, fifty years, a hundred years, dead man.

ARTIE

Gimme the fuckin thing! Toss it over.

LEO

No way, I don't toss a death list, you're so cool, it's like the Nam wall, or the holocaust list, dead, man dead. I'm not gonna touch that. A fuckin list of the dying, soon to be dead. I don't touch that shit. Everyone in that book will be dead. You can't deny that.

ARTIE
(*Grabbing phone book*)

Lemme see it, now.

LEO

You can't deny it.

ARTIE

I can't, okay.

LEO

Okay. The death list.

ARTIE

Lemme see now. E, E, E, Excavations, no, no, Engravers, no, Ergonomic Consultants, fuck, what is that, Envelopes, and, right here, right now, Escort Service…Here we go…We're on it Leo. We are there.

LEO
The old guy was screaming, then he just fell down, he had a box, like a cake box from the bakery, you know with that bakery string... it's so damn strong, you carry the whole cake by the string, you know... you could strangle a person with that shit, this red and white spiral...

ARTIE
"Beautiful models, discreet and confidential", did you hear that Leo, "discreet and confidential." It's right here, beautiful models.

LEO
Please, no. Oh please, please stop them, please man...

ARTIE
Just cool out, we're gonna stop them, there is nothing to be afraid of, god damn it. Except fuckin life. I'm gonna spend every cent I've saved, workin in that death hole. For you, this is for you, cause I love you, you understand. You're okay, we're gonna have some fun dammit, I love you Leo. We served time together. Look at it, (*Monolith*) it's a geometric pattern of perfection, it's not a symbol of God, it is God. We have it made.

LEO
I can't move.

ARTIE
Leo you're on your feet, you're up, you're moving, don't start with the chair shit, so you mugged a guy ten years ago, big deal.

LEO
You call this moving, you really call this moving, what I'm doing is moving?

ARTIE
Yes, I call what you're doing moving, in fact you're animated.

LEO
Animated.

ARTIE
Yeah, animated. You should have been a quarterback. You could have been a killer quarterback.

LEO
Don't call me that, a fuckin quarter of nothing.

ARTIE
It's football man, it's a fucking football term. The most important guy on the team.

LEO
You really want to hurt me, don't you, hurt my feelings, you know why?

ARTIE
Give me the phone.

LEO
Because it makes you feel like a big deal, to fuckin hurt me, hurting me feeds you.

ARTIE
Gimme the fuckin phone.

LEO
I know the guy died, I saw his eyes, I didn't want to kick his head in but I did. Look out, look out man!

ARTIE
Yeah, this one, "Liberated Escort Service", Friendly, Beautiful, Escorts. Or this one, The "Sophisticates". Exotic dates, the city's most beautiful models. "Liberated," I like that one. Leo, I'm dialing. Liberated means free, free models, with free open minds.

LEO
Oh man, oh man…oh man…

ARTIE
Yeah… yeah… beautiful models with open minds.

LEO
He was taking a cake home, you get it, well, Artie a fuckin cake on the sidewalk…Oh man, oh man…Get it out of here, the guy's eyes, I never ever saw anything like that look…what are you doin man…?

ARTIE
I'm on hold…models Leo, models.

LEO
I took his wallet and kicked his head in, he was old, like he was made out of paper, eighty or ninety dollars in the wallet, unfucking believable… kicking his head in…and these fucking things eat me… for that one mistake…one…

ARTIE
Yeah Leo, I think you made more than one mistake…
(*On phone*) Yes…yes… My business acquaintance and I would like some escorts for the evening…No we haven't done business with you before, yeah sure…I'll wait.

LEO
Artie no cake, okay, okay…okay…

ARTIE
I'm on hold…they're playing music…disco stuff…You want to hear it? Listen man…(*to phone*) Yes, Marcia, yes well…Marcia.

LEO
Marcia, Jesus man…Marcia, like fuckin Martians, I don't need any Martians, I don't want to make love love to any Martian shit…

ARTIE
Me?…Yeah, Brimstein, Arthur Brimstein, yeah, two escorts…credit card number…I'd like to pay cash, discreet…Yes I do, well thank you for understanding, three hundred, sure that's fine, we'll cover the cabs

ARTIE, continued
both ways of course. Models, these are models…good, but not too thin, dinner and cocktails, yeah, yeah we're white…white girls will be fine, no not too short…well, we're in rubbish removal, yes it is very lucrative.

LEO
Oh man, Oh man, Oh man, Oh man…

ARTIE
Shut up Leo, don't screw this up. (*to phone*) I understand they're not prostitutes. We may order in. Yes, eighteenth street, four-thirty-four, we're buying the building. Buy, renovate, sell, soon as possible, yes it was an afterthought, 849-3275, yeah, as soon as they walk in I'll hand them the cash, I understand, these are dangerous times. Yes I'll hold…This is cool music, here listen, it's cool…

LEO
Artie, so I ran, with the money, this cake box dying on the street, old cake box, I had on these brown leather shoes, kicked his head in, white box blue string, forty-three bucks, no ninety bucks or ninety-three, not too bad what's happening, what, you're trying to kill me, you don't have any friends, do you, you don't know any girls, you don't know shit…

ARTIE
I'm on hold, just shut up, we need company, new faces.

LEO
Artie, that's your Mexico money. Don't do it, you saved that, man. Five years to save it, get away while you can, I'm dyin, it's cool, just go, okay?

ARTIE
Leo, shut up man, she's back. (*To phone*) Yes, yes Marcia, I'm still here, it's okay…Lori and Tess, blond and brunette. I understand tipping is permissible, these are models…beautiful models…I understand… yes cash. That sounds great…I'm sure we will. Take care. (*Hangs up*) Well Leo, it's done, they are on their way.

LEO

Lock the door, shut off the lights, no, don't shut off the lights.

ARTIE

So, you want the blond or the brunette, Lori or Tess. Which is it Leo, Leo…
(Phone rings)
Yes, oh…hi Marcia, you check the number…I understand, very reputable. Wait, wait Marcia which is which, blonde, brunette, Tess, Lori…that's funny. I would guess Tess is blonde…Well I can't always be right. Really, that's great, nice doing business with you. *(Hangs up)* Leo, she, Marcia, said they're built, big, we lucked out. So you want Tess or Lori, Leo which is it?

LEO

Get away, fuckin buggers, Jesus.

ARTIE

Which one Leo, Tess or Lori?

LEO

I don't know, I don't know anything.

ARTIE

Lori or Tess, make up your fuckin mind.

LEO

Okay, okay, Tess, yeah Tess.

ARTIE

Okay my friend, you got Tess, it's done.

LEO

No, no, no, Lori. I'll take Lori.

ARTIE

Good, Lori the blonde for Leo. Two "L's" Lori, Leo.

LEO
I'm out of here, no, no, I can't.

ARTIE
We have dates Leo, fuckin dates. Get the money, you know the stash.

LEO
I'll get the money, yeah.

ARTIE
Five hundred bucks. I can't touch money, in the paint can Leo. Ten fifty dollar bills. So listen man, you know where the envelopes are.

LEO
Yeah.

ARTIE
Three hundred in one, then a hundred and two fifties in the other two.

LEO
Artie, that's for Mexico. LOOK OUT MAN, LOOK OUT!

ARTIE
Do it man. I'll get to Mexico without the damn money. Leo, pleasure cures, I've done a lot of fuckin reading about this, I've got a theory, you're so fucking animated, calm down okay.

LEO
Don't call me that, animated, animated.

ARTIE
I'm sorry Leo.

LEO
You're damn right you are, you son-of-a-bitch, I've got to lay down. I'll take Tess, Tess the whore.

ARTIE
They're not prostitutes. Escorts, Leo, Escorts.

LEO
Yeah well Tess sounds like a whore to me.

ARTIE
And that's the date you want.

LEO
Yeah, Tess the whore. High Tess, High Test Tess. Artie I want to die, you understand, before the girls get here, I want to fuckin hang myself, shoot my head off, blow it all away, I'm tired man.

ARTIE
You think I'm mister fuckin positive, once you're dead, you're dead man, nothing, not a thing is goin on, nothing, not even black, not even zero, zero is a fuckin idea, nothing, man, Leo nothing, pain, fuckin unhappiness is better than nothing, so we're gonna hang out with some models. I'm sorry about your mugging deal, sorry your dad blew his brains out, too bad, too fuckin bad, I know your story inside out, and stories are bullshit, jive fuckin bullshit. Your kids in the fire, I know Leo, I didn't have it any better, so we have some fun. Breathe some perfumed air, get some pussy. Why die, we'll die anyway.

LEO
Artie, I don't know, I'm screwed man. I don't know what's going on, I can't even fuckin drink, nothing works, nothing, drugs, nothing. I don't know about pussy. I'm so fuckin ugly, who's gonna love me. Gimme a gun man, right through the head, one shot.

ARTIE
Leo, I'm paying these babes, you understand.

LEO
Artie, I'm fucked. I don't understand anything.

ARTIE

I'm paying these girls my life savings, so we can have some fun, a fuckin' double date. Now stop freaking out.

LEO

Artie, I see things that scare me, are they there, I don't fuckin know, Jesus, it's like a stealth bomber shooting these rays at me, all over me.

ARTIE

We gotta clean up, we got to look good, or else they'll leave, Leo just listen, this is all we need. Will you help me? You got to change your clothes Leo.

LEO

I'm scared man.

ARTIE

Clean up, man, just clean up, you know what we're doing…

LEO

We're dyin…

ARTIE

No man we're taking action, action.

LEO

Okay, okay, you don't have to repeat everything, you do that man, all the time, you say things twice, I'm not stupid or deaf, I'm just morbidly depressed, emotionally paralyzed.

ARTIE

Listen Leo, we just have to…

LEO

Don't gimme a fuckin lecture.

ARTIE

I'm cleaning up this place, we have dates, Tess and Lori, we're gonna send out for Chinese food, fun man, we're havin a party, come on Leo, help me clean up.

LEO
Poison, you want me to eat poison, those places poison people, they hate us.

ARTIE
Pick up your socks and underwear, I swear to God man they'll leave, if they see this shit, models Leo, like in the magazines.

LEO
You won't be happy till I'm dead…fuck man, there's bats in here, look at that…Jesus!

ARTIE
Take these pills, NOW! Take them. Good, good boy Leo, do you think I'm okay, you prick, I'll tell you something, I'm worse than you, way worse, but do you care, NO! You don't care, you're so Leoized all you see is Leo. You ever think about anyone else…

LEO
Get off it.

ARTIE
Do you, no.

LEO
Cut it man.

ARTIE
We're gonna think about these girls, we're gonna be fuckin gentlemen, considerate, say it man…say, "Can I get you anything?"

LEO
Jesus…

ARTIE
I don't give a fuck if you see rattlesnakes going up your ass, or a blood worm going up your dick, screw your hallucinations, say it Leo, I'll kill you man, say it. "Can I get you anything?"

(*Pause*)

LEO

Fuck man, why are you doing this?

ARTIE

SAY IT! (*Pause*) Well?

LEO

Can I get you anything?

ARTIE

That is beautiful, come here.

LEO

Get away from me.

ARTIE

They're gonna be here, we gotta clean up.

LEO

Clean up, (*Coming at ARTIE in a violent way*) Clean up! Oh, can I get you anything, can I rip your throat out, I'll smash your head in, to save you from the devil monster escorts.

ARTIE

Get off me, man, get off me…

LEO

I'll clean you all over this pig floor, you killed my kids, you left the hot lit butt in the basement, you said we'll go get some more beer and bourbon, you set the fire, on the pool table, I'll kill you man…

ARTIE

Leo, snap out man, snap out.

LEO

Yeah, yeah, yeah…it's all bullshit, isn't it Artie? Poor old cake box guy.

ARTIE

It's past Leo, you can't change it, it's all how you perceive it, that's all it is, man.

LEO

Fuck…fuck, fuck, fuck…

ARTIE

Yeah I know…

LEO

That's all it is.

ARTIE

Help me with this crap…if you want to, only if you want, man.

LEO

What's their names?

ARTIE

Who?

LEO

The dates, our dates.

ARTIE

Tess and, and…Lori.

(Knock on door)

LEO

Oh man, oh man.

(Knock again)

Let's blow it off, please man. Artie don't do this to me, let's just get the TV fixed, Artie…

ARTIE

Yeah I'm comin.

LEO

Please Artie.

TESS
(*At door*)
Hello, I'm from the agency, I think you have something for me…I'm Tess.

ARTIE

Yeah, hi, I'm Artie, come in, yeah, won't you please come in.

TESS

You need to give me something first.

ARTIE

Yeah, yeah, sure, one second, where's your friend…

TESS

She's on her way…this is the right place.

ARTIE

Yeah, yeah it's the right place.

LEO

Jesus, man…

ARTIE

Cool out Leo, just cool out. (*To TESS*) We're just doing a little renovation here, we're buying the building…

TESS

I'm glad to hear it.

ARTIE

Get changed Leo, go in the other room and get changed. Here you go Tess, three hundred…it's all there and there's more. The tenants left this place in bad shape, don't you think, Tess?

TESS

It looks pretty bad.

ARTIE

Yeah it's a real pig sty. My partner's getting cleaned up, he's a great guy, got a head for business, Leo says buy the building and we buy the building, the man has an ear for profit, he hasn't been wrong yet. Listen Tess, he, my partner Leo, he needs to loosen up, have a little fun, you understand.

TESS

Well that's why I'm here, isn't it?

ARTIE

Exactly right, That's why you're here. You're a beautiful girl.

TESS

Thanks, that's very kind.

ARTIE

Well, true is true, my mother loved to say that, true is true. You can't argue with that can you, true is true. Leo!

LEO

(*From other room*)

Yeah, yeah.

ARTIE

He's fastidious, he's got a thing for cleanliness. Let me ask you something Tess, do you like Oriental food?

TESS

As a matter of fact, yes I do.

ARTIE

I hate to admit it but I have a hard time with the chop sticks, what about you?

TESS

I do okay.

ARTIE

Would you like some wine?

TESS
No thanks, that's okay, I'm fine.

ARTIE
Can I get you anything?

TESS
No I'm okay.

ARTIE
Leo!

LEO
Yeah, yeah.

ARTIE
So I hear you're a model.

TESS
That's right.

ARTIE
We'll, like I said, you're very beautiful, sort of…you know…exotic.

TESS
That's very observant.

ARTIE
To tell you the truth we've never called an escort service before. I believe in being honest, don't you?

TESS
Absolutely.

ARTIE
We're so busy with business and all we don't have time to go out and meet people, women, that's why we called the service. So Tess, where's Lori?

TESS

She'll be here.

ARTIE

Let me ask you something, if I'm out of line you tell me, okay.

TESS

Okay.

ARTIE

Well as I understand we have three hours, with two dates, beautiful liberated models. So has our time started or does it start when Lori gets here, if I'm out of line tell me.

TESS

Our time starts when Lori gets here.

ARTIE

So this is sort of free time.

TESS

Exactly.

ARTIE

But she'll be here.

TESS

Yes she will.

ARTIE

Leo!

(*Enter LEO, cleaned up a bit*)

Leo, I was just telling Tess, about how we're buying the building, oh, Leo this is Tess, Tess, Leo. And I was telling Tess how overworked you are.

LEO

Is Tess short for Teresa or Tessa?

TESS

Teresa.

LEO

You know Teresa, we buy buildings all over the city.

ARTIE

I was telling Tess about it…

LEO

I know you were Artie, for Christ sakes I heard you. Do you like cocktails Teresa?

TESS

Yes, but we don't drink on dates, not first dates.

LEO

That's too bad.

Knock on door)

ARTIE

I got it. (*Opening door*) Wow!

LORI

Hello I'm Lori. The clock is running. (*To TESS*) Sorry I'm late babe. Jesus what is this hole, my God.

TESS

(*To Lori*) I have the cash. (*To men*) So gentlemen, let's go.

LORI

Dinner.

ARTIE

That's not possible, I thought Marcia explained. We're expecting a phone call from Japan, I hope you're not disappointed, but it's a big real estate deal, we can't miss the call.

LORI

Call forwarding. (*Guys look mystified*) Have the call forwarded to the restaurant.

ARTIE

All our papers and stuff are here, we can't forward.

LORI

It's not gonna work.

ARTIE

Lori, you are amazingly beautiful, both of you should be movie stars. Leo could make a call and have you both in the movies in five minutes. We are well connected. Leo.

LEO

Well connected.

LORI

You know what I think, I think you're a couple of bums, in fact I'm surprised your phone works, I think you're on the last leg of your journey and you just want to hang out with some beautiful young women before you kill yourselves for being such terrible failures.

(*Long silence*)

LEO

Jesus.

ARTIE

Fuck.

TESS

Lori, give me a cigarette. That doesn't mean we hate you. You've paid your last bucks, haven't you?

ARTIE

No, we have more money. We have lots of money. Leo?

LEO
We have lots of money.

ARTIE
You hear that, ladies. Buy, renovate, resell, that's our motto.

LEO
I can't, I can't do this man, fuck this, I'm sorry Artie, I'm not good at this, it's makin me sick.

LORI
We're gonna leave.

ARTIE
Hey! Hey! I gave Tess here three hundred dollars.

LORI
Tess, give him his money back and let's get out of here.

TESS
No, I'm not givin any money back.

ARTIE
Listen, it's okay, don't leave, please ladies, whatever you do please don't go. Lori, Tess is right, we're gonna be okay, isn't that right? Leo, Leo…

LEO
Sure Artie, run it down, just run it down.

ARTIE
Okay, we're all okay (*Pause*) So what kind of music do you like… well…

TESS
I like the old stuff, Sinatra, you know, songs.

ARTIE
Songs, yeah, Leo, you like songs.

LEO

Jesus man, songs, I forgot about songs.

ARTIE

Leo don't fuck this up, you fuck this up and I'll kill you, I swear to God.

LORI

Where's the rest room?

ARTIE

It's out in the hall. You're not gonna leave, are you?

LORI

No, I'm not gonna leave.

ARTIE

How about you leave your coat here, that's a beautiful coat, what do you think, Leo?

LEO

Yeah, that's quite a coat.

ARTIE

Lori, listen. (*Taking LORI aside*). Listen, he's an unhappy guy, he works too hard, he's a good guy, he needs some fun, we need to cheer him up, you know. (*Hands her envelope*). We'll have a good time, okay?

LORI

Okay, what's your name?

ARTIE

Artie, and he's Leo. You gonna powder your nose?

LORI

Something like that.

ARTIE

I bet you have some good stuff.

LORI
Excuse me?

ARTIE
I didn't mean anything, we might go in on it, you know.

LORI
Excuse me. (*Exit LORI*)

ARTIE
So Tess, you like Asian food, you know, Oriental.

TESS
Yeah, I like it okay.

ARTIE
Well we got one of the best take out places right around the block.

TESS
We like to go to restaurants.

ARTIE
Well, they don't have any tables in this place, only take out and we're expecting this phone call, from Japan, so we're gonna call out and order in.

TESS
Let's get something clear, Marcia told you we're not prostitutes.

ARTIE
Yes she did, we understand that.

TESS
Ask your friend.

ARTIE
Leo, you understand, these women are not prostitutes.

LEO
I get it, Artie.

ARTIE
But we can dance, right?

TESS
Dance.

ARTIE
Yeah, put on the radio, some songs and dance.

TESS
Is that really what you want?

ARTIE
Leo?

LEO
Yeah that's good, some dancing, we can dance naked, some tribal ritual stuff.

TESS
I don't think so.

ARTIE
You don't think Lori left, do you?

TESS
I don't think so. (*Pause*) You guys, you guys, my father was like you guys, I hated that he was so weak, but I get it now, it isn't weakness, is it Leo, Artie?

LEO
I am weak Tess, I don't play the market, our TV is broken. I don't work on the docks or in a fucking shoe store, I wish I could, I can't. I'm unlovable, I have nothing to offer. Nothing.

(*ARTIE looks in the hall for LORI*)

TESS
Well you could, I mean be giving. Like be giving to children, do you have any kids, Leo?

LEO
No. My kids died in a fire, my wife too.

TESS
Oh, Leo.

LEO
It happened, it's over with.

TESS
I'm sorry, Leo…

LEO
Bad luck, bad fucking luck. I had some bad luck.

TESS
Leo, I'm sorry, I am. I've had bad luck too, I don't need to tell you the details, if you want me to I will.

LEO
It's okay, don't, okay.

TESS
I don't know how to judge whose bad luck is worse. It doesn't really matter, does it?

LEO
I guess not. We keep a tape measure around here, you know, you know, for that kind of shit, you know what I mean?

TESS
Were you happy, with your wife and kids?

LEO
I don't know, I can't think about it. I gave it up, in my head, with every thing else. She was like you Tess, nice. When you have an empty head things come in, uninvited things.

TESS
Your friend Artie here takes good care of you, doesn't he?

LEO
Yeah I guess so, he's okay. (*Pause*) If I let you in Tess, I won't be able to let you out, you'll be everything and things'll be worse.

TESS
You think so?

LEO
Yeah, I know so.

TESS
You might be right, but you might be wrong.

(*Pause*)

LEO
Artie tried to fuck the sky.

TESS
How'd he make out?

LEO
Not too good, it only went a few inches.

TESS
That happens. But he tried.

LEO
Yeah.

TESS
You can't give up trying.

LEO
Why not, if you always fail.

TESS
I don't know Leo, it keeps us going.

LEO
I'm not going. You, Lori, Artie are going, I'm not going, no go-ness. But I'm onboard, like cargo, like a fucking bomb on a vacation plane full of families coming home from Hawaii. You get it Tess, I can't look at you anymore, okay?

TESS
Why?

LEO
I just can't, okay?

TESS
Okay.

(*Enter ARTIE*)

ARTIE
You sure she didn't leave?

TESS
I don't know, I don't think so. She wants to go out for dinner, I don't blame her, that's what a date is.

ARTIE
Listen, we can't leave, do you understand that, no leaving, we need to get that phone call, we have a fucking radio, and we're sending out for Chinese food, okay, you've been paid, so cut the going out stuff.

(*Enter LORI singing*)

LORI
I like New York in June, how about you? I like a Gershwin tune how about you…
(*Picking up LEO to dance*)
You know, you're cute, come on, come on, move your feet.

TESS
What are you doing? I told Marcia I didn't want to work with you.

LORI
Well baby, tough shit, *Holding hands in a movie show, when all the lights are low...*

ARTIE
Girls, no fighting, or is this part of it, I mean to turn us on? I mean so we pay more, or tip more? Leo, Leo! It's all planned out, so it doesn't get dull, these are professionals, professional women. The best. The fighting is part of it, right?

TESS
Right.

LORI
Tess dear, we have the money, so enjoy.

TESS
Artie, you want to see a lesbian fight, is that what you want, that costs a lot of money, you want that?

LEO
No, no fighting, please.

ARTIE
How much?

LEO
No fighting.

ARTIE
How much?

LORI
Five hundred. Here boys, here's a little piece, a little sample. Stand up, I'll rip you apart, Tess, stand up, I hate you, I hate the way you look, the way you smell, I'm gonna rip you apart, I'm gonna stick some

LORI, continued

thing up your ass that's gonna make you cry, lift up your skirt so I can rip your underwear off, cute little bitch. CUT! Five hundred boys.

LEO

Oh man. Artie, please man.

ARTIE

Ladies, discreet is the word of the day, this is not something that can show up on our credit cards, this is cash we're talking about.

LEO

I want her man, I want to see this, please Artie.

ARTIE

I don't have another five hundred, fuck man, you understand that?

LEO

I love this woman, please man.

ARTIE

Which one?

LEO

Mine, Tess. I tell you, Jesus, I'm in love, I want to see them fight.

LORI

So boys, what's going on?

ARTIE

Logistics, conferencing.

LEO

Tess, I love you, you have a goodness in your soul, I'm not a bad guy, I'm really not. I see that goodness. I respect that goodness. I could take care of you.

ARTIE
Leo.

TESS
You've had a rough time, haven't you honey?

LEO
Yeah, it's been bad, up and down, you know, up and down.

TESS
But mostly down, is that right?

LEO
No, not mostly either.

TESS
You want to kiss me, on the cheek, for the bad times? You like Willie Nelson?

LEO
I don't know him, I don't know who he is.

TESS
You don't, do you?

ARTIE
No.

TESS
You want to kiss me on the cheek, for the bad times?

LEO
Sure, yeah. (*Kisses her cheek*)

TESS
You know Leo, we could be friends, close friends, you have soft lips, did anyone ever tell you that?

LEO
No.

TESS
But it could take some gratuities, some giving, on your part.

LEO
Like what?

TESS
Oh, like a few hundred, it's paper honey, only paper, paper for sweet love. I like you Leo, I like you a lot.

LEO
Artie, come on, please. We need more cash. The girls need it. I don't see the flying things, I'm okay now, as long as they don't ever leave.

ARTIE
Come here, come here. Leo! (*Pulls him away*)

LEO
Teresa, excuse me.

ARTIE
There is no more cash.

LEO
You gotta have it, you have another hundred, we can't let them leave, look at me I'm okay, you were right man.

ARTIE
They're not leavin yet.

LEO
They're gonna leave man, sooner or later.

ARTIE
Yeah, sooner or later, we got some time.

LEO
No, you don't understand, they're not leavin, ever.

ARTIE
There's no more money, now have a good time.

LEO
No man, this isn't gonna end.

LORI
What's going on gentlemen?

LEO
You hear that, fuckin gentlemen.

ARTIE
Everything's fine ladies. A little conference.

LEO
They're not leaving, ever.

ARTIE
Okay Leo, whatever you say.

LORI
So what's this thing? (*Monolith*)

LEO
It's God, it's…

ARTIE
It's our manufacturing project, it's the new symbol for all the religions of the world, you know, the Crucifix, the Torah, Buddha, all of it. This covers it all.

LORI
Really.

ARTIE

Oh yeah, it's gonna unite the world, world peace, ya know. We're gonna make them in Japan, that's the call we're waiting for, the final quote, we'll be set for life, so will the world, see it's not male or female, it has no race or anything, it's all inside the monolith, everything.

LEO

Yeah like the Orgone box, the Skinner box, it's some kind of rectangle, with like a geodesic thing happening. We're selling billions of them, so we can't miss that call.

ARTIE

So we gotta order out.

TESS

It's a nice looking thing.

LEO

Thanks, Tess.

ARTIE

What do you think, Lori?

LORI

It's nice all right. I'm a Scientologist.

LEO

You hear that Artie, the Church of Scientology, Dianetics. It's in there too.

LORI

That's pretty fantastic.

LEO

It's big, this is big. And you know what ladies, if it's okay with my partner here, you two are gonna get the first two off the production line. What do you think, Artie?

ARTIE

Yeah sure.

TESS
Really?

ARTIE
Yeah.

LEO
But we're not gonna number them, cause that would make one better than another and that's what we don't want. They're all gonna be the same size, the same material, no gold ones, no diamonds or extra crap, all equal and all. It's bigger than the Internet.

TESS
Really.

ARTIE
It's bigger than the birth of Christ.

LORI
That's pretty big, don't you think, Tess?

TESS
Oh yeah.

LEO
Yeah, you both could be like the Virgins Mary, written up in some new Bible type thing.

ARTIE
Yeah, the heroic women who ordered in. Because you are Goddesses, you are.

LEO
You really are. Let's be honest okay, for a minute, okay?

LORI
Go.

TESS

Okay.

ARTIE

You came here to make some money, right?

TESS

Right.

LEO

We know that.

ARTIE

So you made your money, so, so, (*Pause*) So fuck off!

LEO

No Artie, please no, please Artie…

ARTIE

No, we don't need this, to suck up to some money sucking broads, because we're so down, and you look so good, get out, fuck this, you have our money, so go do whatever you do with it, what do you do, buy dope or clothes, or new fuckin shoes, or crack, or what…

LEO

Please Artie. He doesn't mean it, he really doesn't, please don't go, please. What about the girl fight? Artie don't do this, please man.

(*Fight, LEO holds ARTIE down*)

LORI

Listen pricks, you think, oh fuck what you think, or what I do with the grand I make every day, I take care of people, look at me, punks, you think I like this, punk, I have bad habits, okay. I've got my own troubles, okay, I pay the bills and lie everyday about my fucked up life, and I have a kid in a foster home, and it tears my heart out, you hear that, I am a piece of meat, a love object for you idiots who think some piece of ass can save you from the terror of your own uselessness. You always think some nice babe with beautiful tits and a nice ass is

LORI, continued
gonna save you from your piece of shit life, it's a joke, it is beyond stupidity, I see it every night, every day, all the time. You seem like bright guys. As for me, just ask for what you want. I'm trying, I'm trying to get clear.

ARTIE
I told you. Go! Just leave! Just…

LEO
Artie stop, please man, please, please girls, he doesn't mean it. Artie, please, please…

ARTIE
Fuck it man, just fuck it.

LEO
Artie, please. (*Seeing stuff*) Oh man, oh man.

ARTIE
Okay, okay, OKAY! I'm sorry.

LEO
Let's turn our lives over to the monolith, look at it. No wait, just think of it, no more worries, no more problems, only good things, it's all in there, that thing. I'm gonna do it. I give myself to, to the unnamable presence of purity, to you. (*Kneels before monolith. Silence*) There you see. I did it! Now you and you and you, Artie. Am I glowing, am I fucking glowing or am I glowing?

LORI
Tess, what the hell are you doing?

TESS
I'm into it.

LORI
I'm out of here.

LEO
No!

ARTIE
We paid you good money. We paid for escorts, your time's not up.

LORI
You gonna stop me? Hey big boy, you gonna stop me?

ARTIE
Oh yeah, I'm gonna stop you. I'm gonna stop you.

LORI
Son-of-a-bitch. (*Takes out Mace and sprays it at ARTIE*)

ARTIE
God! (*ARTIE grabs her*) Leo, I can't see, Leo, man, I can't fucking see. But I got her. I got you bitch. (*Holding on tight*).

TESS kneeling to Monolith)

LEO
Artie.

ARTIE
Yeah.

LEO
You got her.

ARTIE
Yeah

LEO
She's beautiful, man.

ARTIE
I know that.

LEO

I'm gonna order out.

ARTIE

You got the number?

LEO

Yeah, I'm gonna order big.

ARTIE

Good, order big.

LEO

Lobster and shrimp and shit. I'll ask the guy to pick up wine.

ARTIE

They don't do that.

LEO

Yeah they do.

ARTIE

Good, do it.

LEO

We got more cash?

ARTIE

I don't know, if not we'll kill the fucking guy.

LEO

Yeah. We're omnipotent. (*Phone*) Hello…yeah, Purple Dragon…this is Leo…Oh yeah…434, 18th Street, 3rd floor, yeah here's our order…ready…it's gonna be seafood. Shrimp with mixed vegetables, Shrimp with Cashew nuts, Shrimp with baby corn, Shrimp with hot and spicy sauce, Shrimp with Lobster sauce, Sweet and sour Shrimp, Sha-cha Shrimp, Hunan Shrimp, General Tso's Shrimp, General Tso's Scallops, Hunan Scallops, Shrimp in bird's nest, Lobster in a bird's nest, Lobster Cantonese and some Shrimp rolls, Shrimp fried rice,

                          LEO, continued
Crabmeat sweet and sour, Moo Shu shrimp, Moo Shu Scallops, Fish head soup, eyes in, Crabs in a nest, Dragon Lobster fantasy, Fantail Shrimp, your Orange Dragon mixed seafood platter. And ask the guy to pick up five bottles of white wine and five bottles of red…sure you can…we'll take good care of him, yeah, special customers…bye.

                                ARTIE
Leo! I can't see, Leo.

                                 LEO
I know. You'll be okay.

                                ARTIE
I'm good. (*To LORI*) How long does this shit last?

                                LORI
            (*Trying to talk, ARTIE's hand over her mouth*)
I don't know.

                                ARTIE
Don't scream, it'll freak Leo out, okay?

                                LORI
Okay. (*Removing his hand*)

                                ARTIE
How long am I blind for?

                                LORI
I don't know, it says on the can.

                                ARTIE
Leo, read the can.
                    (*ARTIE tosses can to LEO*)

                                 LEO
I can't read this shit, the print is too tiny.

ARTIE
You keep your glasses so dirty, ask Tess.

LEO
She's giving herself.

ARTIE
What does it take, a fucking year?

LEO
I don't know man. Tess, Tess, she's really into it. We're doin it, man. We're doin good.

LORI
Let me up, I have good eyes.

ARTIE
Yeah you probably have a gun too. Leo, there's a magnifying glass by the toaster.

LEO
I'm lookin man, I'm lookin…,I got it Artie.

ARTIE
Read the can, how long, how long? The magnifier by the toaster. How long am I blind for, I'm blind Leo!

LEO
Okay, okay, I got it, what am I lookin for?

ARTIE
Effect, the effect.

LEO
It doesn't say. Jesus, this stuff was made in Newark. This thing is great, I can read all the details.

ARTIE
How long, Leo how long am I blind for?

LEO
It says, "The assailant, slash, perpetrator can lose eyesight for five or ten minutes." Yeah, five to ten minutes or up to an hour.

ARTIE
Fuck.

LEO
You're gonna miss the girl fight and the food and everything.

LORI
I'm sorry, okay?

ARTIE
Okay.

LORI
I got scared, I felt trapped. Let me go, I'll hold your hand, okay? I'll be nice, Artie, okay.

ARTIE
Okay, we're good guys. My eyes burn bad.

LORI
I know, I'm sorry. I'll hold your hand, I'm sorry. I'll get you a wash cloth, okay?

ARTIE
We're good men.

LORI
You are, I know you are. I just got scared.
        (Getting wash cloth, running water)
Jesus, you got no pressure here.

ARTIE
Yeah it's all screwed up.

LORI
(*Wiping ARTIE's eyes*)

Is that better?

ARTIE

No. (*Pause*) Can I kiss you?

LORI

No.

ARTIE

Why the hell not?

LORI

Because I don't love you, does that make sense?

ARTIE

But if we paid you enough, you would.

LORI

I guess so.

ARTIE

Why do I want to kill you?

LORI

Because I made you blind.

ARTIE

On the cheek?

LEO

You okay, Artie?

ARTIE

No man, I'm not. (*To LORI*) On the cheek.

LORI
Sure Artie, on the cheek, like you'd kiss your aunt. (*ARTIE tries to kiss her hard on the mouth*) You fucker, son of a bitch.

ARTIE
Yeah well let me tell you something, Lori, before this night is over I'm gonna rape you, and you're gonna love it, and when you're an old lady on your death bed, it's gonna be the only significant memory you have. And as the life support systems try to keep you alive, you'll see my face, and my cock as the only interesting thing that ever happened to you. You are a fucking prisoner. Leo!

LEO
Yeah?

ARTIE
Did you order the food?

LEO
I think I did, I don't know.

LORI
You are both going to go to jail, you know that, come on, what is it, mommy didn't like you, poor babies, I'll suck you off, for free, no charge, then your dreams will slide down my face. And you'll be another hopeless piece of nothing.

ARTIE
Leo, lobster, think seafood.

LEO
Yeah, it's comin man. You're sure we have money, Artie?

ARTIE
If we don't, we'll kill the messenger, I mean the delivery boy. This is it, pal. I don't like this fucking blindness.

LORI

I tell you what, we'll buy you guys dinner, the best restaurant in town, on us, you're our dates. We buy...

ARTIE

Bullshit.

LEO

I can't go out, I killed a guy, I'm under house arrest...

ARTIE

Shut up Leo.

TESS

(*After kneeling in front of the monolith*)
I'm saved. I feel better, way better, you guys are something.

LEO

Teresa, you hungry? We got some great stuff on the way.

TESS

Hungry yeah, but better, there's something vibrating inside of it, that thing, what is it, there aren't that many things in nature that vibrate hard and fast, except bees, there's a missing link someplace, something unnatural, why should those speeds do that, that give me so much satisfaction.

LEO

You like Oriental seafood. Shrimp with mixed vegtables, Shrimp with Cashew nuts, Shrimp with baby corn, Shrimp with hot and spicy sauce, Shrimp with Lobster sauce, Sweet and sour Shrimp, Shacha Shrimp, Hunan Shrimp, General Tso's Shrimp, General Tso's Scallops, Hunan Scallops, Shrimp in birds nest, Lobster in a birds nest, Lobster Cantonese and some Shrimp rolls, Shrimp fried rice Crab sweet and sour, Moo Shu shrimp, Moo Shu Scallops, Fish head soup, with the eyes in, Crabs in a nest, Dragon Lobster fantasy, fantail Shrimp... Orange Dragon mixed seafood platter.

TESS
I don't think I can eat living things anymore.

LEO
No Teresa, Tess, they're all cooked, oriental style.

TESS
I don't think I can eat things that were once living. Eyes or no eyes.

LEO
Artie?

ARTIE
What Leo.

LEO
I don't think Tess is gonna eat.

ARTIE
That's pretty sad news.

LEO
Artie, can you see?

ARTIE
A little man, it's blurred, I can see a little, thank God.

LORI
So we can leave, what do you think, you can have your money back, get your TV fixed or get a new one. That okay with you, Tess?

TESS
Yeah, I guess so.

ARTIE
No calling the cops.

LORI

No, never, you're good guys, I mean it.

ARTIE

Leo, what do you think?

LORI

Leo?

LEO

No way man, no fuckin way, I told you before man, when she came in, I didn't see the bats and shit, then when you (*LORI*) came in I knew that that thing (*Monolith*) was real and everything is real, in real time. I can't take any more losses man, no more hits, nobody is leavin, nothin is gonna change. Everybody got that?

TESS

Leo, you want me to stay with you, make it okay, I will, let Lori go, I'll stay with you.

LEO

You hate us, you think we're going to kill you.

TESS

I don't think so, I think you're on to something, I do.

LEO

And you, Lori?

LORI

I think you are on to something, about God. You want me to give myself to that thing.

(*TESS takes out another can of Mace and sprays it all over both men*)

ARTIE

Look out, Leo!

                             LEO

I'm blind, I can't see, I can't see, man, Tess!

   (*WOMEN run out the door, TESS grabs the monolith*)

                             ARTIE

We fucked up.

                             LEO

Artie.

                             ARTIE

Yeah.

                             LEO

I'm scared man. Help me man.

                             ARTIE

I'm trying, I'm trying to see.

                             LEO

I'm blind, Jesus.

                             ARTIE

I got you man.

                             LEO

We fucked up, we screwed it all up, (*Beginning to cry*) so beautiful, weren't they, we lost them, didn't we?

                             ARTIE

We lost them.

                             LEO

Bullshit, I can't man, I can't accept it, bullshit, bullshit, bullshit. (*Getting more and more freaked out*) Please man please. What is the deal, what man, what, I give up, what do you want, what? WHAT! (*Yelling at Monolith that isn't there*) WHAT? WHAT MAN? WHAT? WHAT?

ARTIE

Don't hurt it, Leo, be kind man, forget yourself.

LEO

Did you see her, she was right here. YOU SAW IT MAN!

ARTIE

I did Leo. BEFORE SHE BLEW MY EYES OUT! Where are you Leo?

LEO

I'm here, I'm right here.

(*ARTIE picks up pillow and grabs LEO from behind, puts pillow over LEO'S face and suffocates him*)

ARTIE

You were here Leo, you were definitely here.

(*ARTIE picks up piece of paper, touches it like he's reading braille, finds phone and dials*)

Yeah, I have an order I'd like to cancel…the big one with all the seafood…It's too late, it's on it's way…oh man…no, it's okay.

(*Lights fade, soft light up in doorway. An OLD MAN in a hat and overcoat appears holding a cake box. Soft music up*)

FADE
END OF PLAY

ARNIE GETS IT GOOD

Arnie Gets it Good 1997

First Production, Club Metronome
Burlington, VT
Directed by the Author

Original Cast

Arnie – Paul Schnabel
Lori – Barbara Shatara
Judy – Kelly Jane Thomas
Dr. Steinbeck – Allan Nicholls
Cop – Dennis McSorley
Dr. – Peter Freyne
Van Driver – Dennis McSorley
Frank Sinatra – Allan Nicholls
Man – Peter Freyne

Cast of Characters

Arnie (Gold) – A middle aged man, ex-college professor
Lori – Hot social worke.
Judy – Arnie's wife
Dr Steinbach – Psychiatrist
Cop – A NYC policeman
Gina – A young medical student
Doctor – A doctor
Van Driver – A van driver
Frank – Frank Sinatra
Man – Judy's new boyfriend

Arnie Gets it Good

ARNIE
(Aside to Audience)

I'm telling you I was just sitting there in the employment office. It's like the whole room is on fire, the light level is cranked, there's flames coming out of people's heads, like their heads are vessels of over-lit emptiness. It's one of those capturing moments and I realize I don't want a job, what I want is money and I want this scrubbed woman who's sitting behind her desk. You know those kind of women? Like the ones who work in banks, they always look like they just came out of the shower, like too clean, like I have all these microbes on me and they don't, like my microbes could infect them and make them human.

So this micro-clean babe calls my name, I mean the room is swinging in white light, like I can see through her clothes and into the all not knowing head. She's looking at my application, like I haven't had a job in at least ten, twelve years and I don't want one now, what I want is money and I want this babe behind the desk to take me home and make me a seafood dinner, like these handsome rays are shooting out from my inner soul. So I say to her, what's your name. She says Lori, I say Lori, I don't want a fuckin' job, I want you to take me back to your clean apartment, give me a warm bath, make me dinner, some steamed shrimp deal with a light French wine, make love to me and let me sleep between clean sheets for three or four days and watch your cable connected Sony around the clock. The French Open is on, red clay. I got wiped out in the first round at Wimbledon. Do you play tennis Miss Campbell or just sit on your ass all day? Now fuckin' Lori looks a little pissed off.

LORI

Mr. Gold, your work history looks a little suspect. There are gaps. It says here you were a research scientist for twenty-five years.

ARNIE

To find out how shit works, the human experimenter trying to get it, understanding the human psyche and the universe of pulsating radiation waves.

LORI

The opening we have is for a warehouse worker, loading trucks.

ARNIE

I can't do that, my back is all fucked up. I can't lift. Listen Lori, I really like you, I could do great things for you. You're so clean and hot. And you're in the white light, bathed in it, it means something. Where do buy your clothes, it must cost you a fortune. Lori you don't need it, the fuckin' clothes. I can tell, you're an artist, a thinker, like me.

LORI

Mr Gold, I'd appreciate it if you didn't use profanities.

ARNIE

What do you mean?

LORI

Your language.

ARNIE

You want me to speak French or fuckin' German, yo hablo Espanol?

LORI

That's very good, we'll call you if anything comes up.

ARNIE

Really, I have no phone. How the fuck are you going to call me? Now, what about you and me?

LORI

This interview is over.

ARNIE
(Aside)
Now she's hot only because she's so repressed, you know those kind of women, like they have to stay perfect. I know she's attracted to me, but screw her and her fuckin' list of shit jobs. So I hang outside the building waiting for her to come out for lunch. I keep thinking about taking her clothes off and I'd be careful not to get them wrinkled, tight little nipples and smooth skin in this little perfect apartment with little tissue box holders and a fuckin' terry cloth toilet seat cover. I just want to tell her she doesn't need that shit. She's at that goddamn desk all day to buy crap she never needed in the first place. You know, what a waste. She could be a goddam movie star or something.

Now, I wait outside the building on Eighth Avenue for her to come out for lunch. You know, to give her some information so she doesn't fuck up her life with bullshit. Maybe she'd take me out to lunch, these chicks always have some kind of eating disorder, like she probably chews each mouthful of food a million times. I could live on the food they leave on their plate. Now I don't want to scare her. She could think this crazy fuck wants to hurt her or something.

Right at twelve noon this river of people comes out, like when a movie gets out, I don't get that, it's fuckin' stupid, everybody doing everything at the same time. Be at work at nine, eat lunch at twelve, leave work at five. Always stuck in a crowd. I could fix the whole thing, stagger the shit, I'm good at that. It's like droves of cosmetics pouring out of these indestructible structures. What's the deal with that? So I spot her, what's cool is she's taller than I thought, something so hot about tall women. Those legs wasted behind a desk.

ARNIE

Excuse me, Lori. Just give me a minute. I have some information for you, I'm not trying to hurt you, no don't just walk away like I'm not here, I'm a good guy, can I just walk with you. I'll walk with you okay? Lori?

LORI

No.

ARNIE

Look at this sunlight, do you know how far the sun is from Earth, it's

ARNIE, continued

really far and without it we'd freeze right up, in a millisecond, all ice. You're not ice, are you? You don't need that crummy job. You could be a movie star. Come on, baby.

ARNIE
(Aside)

Well that was the end of that, maybe I got too heavy too fast, she just disappeared into the flow, into one of those stupid restaurants. They had the menu in the window, a tuna salad sandwich, six-fifty. Six dollars and fifty cents, I don't get it. Tuna and a cup of coffee probably comes to ten bucks, Jesus! And she probably drinks that two dollar bottled fuckin' tap water, she probably sat behind the desk for over an hour to earn the money to buy some shit lunch, in a couple of years it'll give her a fat ass and she'll waste fifty bucks on some tight buns video tape. I don't know what I said wrong. Chicks drive me nuts.

ARNIE

Excuse me, Lori. Just give me a minute. I have some information for you, I'm not trying to hurt you, no don't just walk away like I'm not here, I'm a good guy, can I just walk with you. You got a nice ass, for now, don't waste it in that creep hole fluorescent office. I just want to enlighten you to something.

LORI

No.

ARNIE

Do you know how far the sun is from Earth, it's really far and without it we'd freeze right up. You're not ice are you?

LORI

Leave me alone or I'll call the police.

ARNIE

Yeah, well screw you.

ARNIE
(Aside)
I was in this tiny hotel room on the lower east side, but I was evicted today, I don't know what to do. I'm not a criminal; I can't rob someone or someplace, I would have liked to gone into that place and rubbed their fuckin' tuna salad in their fat ugly faces, and emptied the register, but I'm a nice guy. Sometimes I think I've lost my charm, looks, everything, I wish I wasn't fuckin' born, I want to lay down and die, but this fire of life won't let me. I can't panhandle, not that I haven't done it, I hate that pleading shit. No money, no friends, no anything. And God lets me walk around and kills little kids with all kinds of horrible disease crap, where the fuck is that truth?
Yeah well I'm going to change it right now. I'm not stupid, damn it, damn it, damn it. If only my mind could understand my mind, make some fuckin' sense out of it. Damn it! Damn it! Damn it!

(Woman enters. It's ARNIE's wife, JUDY)

JUDY
I love you babe.

ARNIE
I love you too.

JUDY
Everything is going to be okay, better than okay. I'm spinning with your love.

ARNIE
I'm spinning too. I respect you.

JUDY
I respect you too.

ARNIE
Yeah, that's good, except Judy, I'm all fucked up.

JUDY
I know, it's okay, it's part of your charm.

ARNIE
I don't get it, the whole deal, I just don't get it.

JUDY
You don't need to, no one gets it.

ARNIE
Then why do they act okay?

JUDY
That's what we do. Like the birds and the clouds. Just float, honey. It's fine not to get it.

ARNIE
I'm not okay, am I?

JUDY
You're perfect, you make me happy, just being near you makes me happy, makes me feel more alive.

ARNIE
I don't know how to live or think, my mind goes off.

JUDY
Just do something simple. Don't think so much, listen to the radio, watch TV, buy a car, get a dog.

ARNIE
It doesn't interest me. So I make you feel good?

JUDY
You let me feel good.

ARNIE
I mean sexually.

JUDY
I know what you mean, you give me space to feel good.

ARNIE

See, I don't understand that.

JUDY

You don't need to.

ARNIE

Yeah, but I do.

JUDY

Yeah, but you don't. I love you for your disturbed way of being.

ARNIE
(Aside)

Now, I had lots of opportunities to do good. I had this interest in graphics, the design of things on a page. I would look at a page in the newspaper or a magazine, then blur my eyes, pull back the corners like I was oriental and look at the construction of the page. That's all I could do. I went for this one job designing wallpaper. They made me a wallpaper inspector, what the fuck is that, looking for imperfections in the repeated patterns. I had like this hand crank, there were about two feet between the takeup roller and the output roller, between two rollers was my window of opportunity, it was really disturbing and boring, after two days I never found one mistake, I felt really useless, so I quit.

I got about fifty bucks and I bought this woman, Elaine, I thought I was in love with Elaine, so I bought her a watch, she threw it at me the same day I gave it to her, so I stomped it into the sidewalk, all these mini details about time. Don't think I didn't cry, because I did. The little clock work in with the worms. If only my mind would shut up. I tried drinking but it only made me sick. I tried smoking pot but I got even more scared and confused.

Now I've applied to this TV game show, the Wheel, I go to this bar at seven every night and I get the fucking puzzle right off, before any letters are even up. Now Vanna's a babe I'd like to have, she is hot and probably fuckin' rich. See, that's my last hope, the Wheel. There is some luck involved and I'd probably get fucked. Sorry Arnold, lose

ARNIE, continued
a turn, or fuckin' bankrupt. I don't have good luck. Elaine left me because I couldn't function and had bad luck, I told her that up front. Then one day Judy says:

JUDY
Arnie, you can't function and you have bad luck.

ARNIE
Yeah, well I told you that up front.

JUDY
Yeah but you really can't function and you never said anything about the bad luck.

ARNIE
I told you Judy, I really can't function and you said…

JUDY
Of course you can.

ARNIE
No I can't.

JUDY
But you're good in bed, that's functioning.

ARNIE
Yeah well that's all. A mosquito can fuck.

JUDY
Arnie, I don't think mosquitoes make love, they fertilize and that's all I need.

ARNIE
That's not all of it. That's not all I need.

JUDY
That's all I need, we'll be fine.

ARNIE
(Aside)
And Arnie, what kind of name is that, that's bad fuckin' luck. Arnie, Arnold.

JUDY
We'll be fine.

ARNIE
(Aside)
I say okay, then she throws me out, I mean twelve years later. I had a bad night, one bad night twelve times 365, 4,380 nights not counting leap years, then one bad night she says:

JUDY
Arnie, you have to leave tomorrow.

ARNIE
(Aside)
What the fuck is that? I wake up, she's out of the apartment and all my stuff is in shopping bags in the hallway. So I toss it all down the incinerator with my keys, the key ring has this little plastic piece of shit picture of a guy in a Porsche convertible with his hair all flowing, like in the Maxell tape ad. I can imagine the distortion of the thing all melting in the incinerator turning into some devil-like creature floating down a river of garbage, headed towards the falls with a semi hard-on in his hand and a tiny half smile on his face. I told her on our second date:

ARNIE
Judy, sweetheart, I have no ambition. I don't understand ambition.

JUDY
Arnie, you're an existentialist, like Sartre and Camus, it's okay, you just don't understand how to define yourself.

ARNIE
(Aside)
So I tell her:

ARNIE

At least those guys wrote books, I mean I'm not a fuckin' idiot. I know who those guys are, I'm not a fuckin' jerk, I'm a professor.

JUDY

You don't need to write books, you're you. Just be you.

ARNIE
(Aside)

Then she throws me out, I mean twelve years later, because of one bad night, what's the deal with that?

JUDY
(Aside)

The thing is, he was out of control. It started with little things, like changing things in the dish cabinet, one day by color then by size, then by use, then with eating utensils, like I'm not a freak about that stuff. One day he says: I'm on to something, I came home and he had all the forks and spoons and knives lined up like little armies or chess pieces, on the tile kitchen floor and he was sitting in the middle of the floor all crying, tears dripping, into a little tear puddle, he just looked at me and said: this is what it's all about, it's so damn sad, the way it works it's so sad.

Now we had two subscriptions to magazines, I had one to Vogue, him to Scientific American. He stayed up all night and with his barber scissors that I bought him, I mean you don't use barber scissors on paper, it ruins the cutting edge. So he cuts out all these semi-exposed breasts in the Vogue and these diagrams in Scientific American, all about weather and DNA and uses my whole-wheat flour to glue them all over the living room wall and ceiling. I begged him to go into treatment, he said: I'm on to something.

ARNIE

I'm on to something.

JUDY
(Aside)

Then he stopped going to work, he was teaching up at Columbia, he stopping shaving and bathing, and sleeping in our bed, except every

JUDY, continued

few weeks he'd run a bath and stay in it for days, never running any more hot water, he'd be shivering, playing with this wind up frog that would do this frog kick around the tub. I said: Arnie you need some help. He said:

ARNIE

We don't need any help, okay? I'm on to something.

JUDY
(Aside)

The pages of Scientific American floating in the tub, like little islands, I was worried he'd freeze to death or flood the whole building. So he agreed to go to a shrink. I mean I was afraid to leave the apartment. I wanted him to get help, I think it was his intellect closing in on him. So we went to Doctor Steinbach.

(DR. STEINBACH'S OFFICE)

ARNIE

I'm on to something, a breakthrough and Judy can't understand. I waited for this for a long time.

JUDY

I'm afraid of him, not that he will hurt me, but, it's like it's not him, he's lost his job teaching.

ARNIE

I can't teach, there's nothing left to teach, nothing. I want to say it in one sentence, then class over, college over, then hand out diplomas.

DR. STEINBACH

And what would that sentence be?

ARNIE

The truth, the whole truth is…blah, blah, blah.

DR. STEINBACH
And that's it?

ARNIE
Yeah, no more comparative religion or ultra math or fuckin' Greek literature, none of that shit, like here it is and go have a happy honest life. But I couldn't fill in the blah, blah, blah.

DR. STEINBACH
Do you want to die Arnie?

ARNIE
No, never. I want to live forever. I want to break through. Like Salk or Pasteur or Freud or Baba. I am on to something.

JUDY
Doctor…

DR. STEINBACH
And what are you on to?

ARNIE
The nature of truth, I'm on to it. I'm about to pin it, right to the wall. Truth, motherfucker!

DR. STEINBACH
Well Arnie, that's pretty big.

ARNIE
No shit it's big! And don't call me Arnie, Mister Arnold Gold, Golden, Silver, and you call me sir, who the hell are you?

DR. STEINBACH
I'm here to help you.

ARNIE
You're a joke, I can tell your brains are in your balls.

DR. STEINBACH
And how can you tell that?

ARNIE
From the way you look at my wife, you're evil. Your electric system confuses you, brains, balls, prick, brains, balls, prick. That's why you have back problems, you do have spine problems don't you? Well, answer! Do you have back problems? Doctor hot shit, do you? You have bad posture. Your wiring is all fucked up.

JUDY
Doctor, last night Arnold marked himself with my lipstick and eyebrow pencils, making all these diagrams and symbols all over his naked body. I stopped him from going outside because I didn't want him in to end up jail. I can't take it anymore.

DR. STEINBACH
Mr. Golden…

ARNIE
Gold!

DR. STEINBACH
Mr. Gold, I'm going to suggest you go to the hospital, Hillside Hospital, for observation, for a week or two.

ARNIE
Do you know the symbols of the Cree or the Mohawk, the Aztec, I'm sure you don't, do you? And stop looking at my wife. Do you know them?

DR. STEINBACH
No, I don't.

ARNIE
You see that, Judy? How in the hell is this fake going to solve anything? Explain that to me.

JUDY
He's trying to understand.

ARNIE
Well he can't, can you, can you, motherfucker?

DR. STEINBACH
There's no need for that.

ARNIE
For what, no need for what?

DR. STEINBACH
For you getting so angry and using that language.

ARNIE
If I don't get angry, who will? Will you?

DR. STEINBACH
No.

ARNIE
Will you Judy, Judith my dear? Will you get angry?

JUDY
No, I'm trying to understand.

ARNIE
No, just accept the bullshit, right? Study the bullshit, teach the bullshit, sell the bullshit. We all go along in our little canoes, paddling up the river of garbage, oh there's a little piece of bullshit, let the next guy pick it up, "I'm headed towards the source in my nice new canoe with my nice little family and screw everyone else. I'm not going to touch shit, it carries disease of the body, of the mind, so I'll crank up the stereo and the TV and keep paddling." That's the deal, isn't it? Well, I don't hear you.

JUDY
You see what I mean doctor?

DR. STEINBACH
Arnold, we're not here to discuss philosophy…

ARNIE
I'm talking about reality, fucking human reality.

DR. STEINBACH
Your reality.

ARNIE
No, The Reality.

DR. STEINBACH
So your reality is the real reality?

ARNIE
You're goddamn right it is.

DR. STEINBACH
And what are you doing about it, besides getting upset?

ARNIE
Nothing, except looking at your ugly face thinking about fucking my wife after you get me locked up…

DR. STEINBACH
Well there's your problem, isn't it?

ARNIE
No, there's your problem.

DR. STEINBACH
Arnold, are you God?

ARNIE
Don't be a fucking idiot, visions of grandeur; I can just see you writing it down, sneaky little prick. The man thinks he's God, lock him up. So you can try to fuck my wife.

DR. STEINBACH
Do you think you should be locked up, are you going to hurt someone?

ARNIE
No, I'll leave that to you.

DR. STEINBACH
Are you going to hurt yourself?

ARNIE
You're doing a pretty good job.

DR. STEINBACH
Do you know you're hurting your wife?

ARNIE
No. I feel she's afraid and confused, but I have never done anything to hurt her.

DR. STEINBACH
Judy, how is Arnold hurting you?

JUDY
I'm afraid and confused; I don't understand his actions. I'm worried about his sanity, my sanity, I feel alone. I'm afraid to sleep, I don't know what he's going to do, I feel I'm in danger.

DR. STEINBACH
Would you like him to leave?

JUDY
Yes. I'd like him to leave and get some help, maybe some medication so we can be together again.

DR. STEINBACH
What do you think Arnold, Mister Gold?

ARNIE
I think you want to fuck my wife, I think you're an arrogant punk who's had life too easy. I think I'm on to something that is far past your understanding. I think I want to smash up your fucking office and slam this chair over your head, but because that would give you reason to lock me up, I restrain myself. I love my wife dearly, she is a gifted, beautiful being.

JUDY
Honey, I love you too. Please accept some help.

ARNIE
I will, I really will. Judy, go down and get a cab, I have something to say to the doctor. Is our time up?

DR. STEINBACH
Yes it is. Take care, Mrs. Gold, next Tuesday.

JUDY
Good. Arnold, I'll see you downstairs.

ARNIE
(Aside)
Then I smashed up the whole fucking place, ripped his phony diplomas off the wall, he was hiding under his desk, he had these art prints on the wall, the abstract expressionists, so neatly framed as if the brilliant artists could afford those fucking frames. The fucker was really scared.
Later that night Judy and I made this hot love, it brought tears to both our eyes. I could see how much she wanted to believe that I was still me. I don't know what that click is, that changes everything, a look in the eyes, a tear on the pillow. One second that makes everything okay. I had one second of okayness. Behind her, on top of her, tears falling, then sleep. Dreams of lost in New York, trying to find home and no home to find. Gangs of bad black killers chasing me up stairs and fire escapes, into closed hallways, black killers cutting my pockets and face, slamming empty glass frames over my head, blood dripping down my face, long manicured fingers tearing at my mouth

ARNIE, continued

and lips, words echoing in an elevator shaft, a steak knife on my throat. Then they pull out their huge black cocks and I slice them one by one, they bow, I pound them and embrace them and toss their cocks into a garden filled with butterflies and dog shit, the dogs there shitting with white teeth smiles and hundreds of Doctor Steinbachs with little plastic sandwich bags picking up the shit and inside the bags the shit turns into money, legal tender and the butterflies, now moths eat away at the doctor's pockets and the sandwich bags and the money and there's Judy in the field alone, except she's floating, looking down at me. There's a bass drum pounding, it's the door. The awake door.

ARNIE

What?

COP

Just come with us.

ARNIE

I haven't done anything.

COP

Arnold, put your hands behind your back.

ARNIE

Why? I had a bad dream.

COP

We're going to take a little ride.

ARNIE

Yeah, ride this. JUDY!

JUDY

Please take him away. I'm sorry Arnie. Honey, I'm sorry.

ARNIE
(Aside)
Well then they take me off, the New York City Police, charming as hell. First to this little lock up, like this little cell, the cool thing is they are all being nice, treating me with respect. I don't get it. It's a horrible thing, being locked up. I don't know what I did.

ARNIE
What did I do? Please tell me.

COP
Your wife said you had a kitchen knife and were about to slit your wrists or your throat if she didn't pretend to be someone…Madonna or someone.

ARNIE
Joan of Arc. I would never hurt her.

COP
We're going to keep you in jail overnight. For her and your protection. Don't worry, Mr. Gold.

ARNIE
(Aside)
I called Judy from jail and told her it was just acting out. That I learned my lesson, to please not leave me in jail, she never came. It became okay, the lockup. Then this big black guy, right in the cell with me says, "You get it, don't you?" Then he takes a leak in the bowl, he says, "I could kill you with one blow, bam, motherfucker, choice, you dig it." There was a sweet ring to the way he says motherfucker. Like the way he said it, to fuck your mother, it had the true ugly meaning in the articulation. Now, I have the best night sleep ever, deep. I hear him scratching notes on some pad, and I hear the notes floating over my dreams, like some forgotten paper music.
In the morning at the arraignment he gets ten years, ten years of hell. I walk free, whatever the fuck that means. He turned and looked at me as if to say or ask; what does it mean? Mother-fucker.

ARNIE, continued

So I'm walking on upper Broadway, did you know Broadway is the longest street in the world? Not quite the Great Wall of China, the Great Wall, the only man-made thing that can be seen from outer space. So I go into this bar up by Columbia University and I meet this old student of mine, he's with this dark haired coed, he's really drunk. And it's like she has this halo around her head. I rub my legs against her knees, and this kid is telling her what a great teacher I am. She's all hot and interested in Buddhism. The kid goes to take a piss and I ask her if she lives in the dorm. She says no, she has her own place. I tell her let's get out of here, after the kid has bought me three drinks. She goes for it. We leave.

ARNIE

So you like older men?

GINA

I don't like anything. You probably couldn't fuck if you tried. Do you still have a prostate? I'm a med student. I cut out a prostate just a few hours ago, from a cadaver, swollen bad. You poor guys. The gland gets bad as you age. Cut it out so you can live and wear diapers, pissing in your pants. No hard-on, nothing. That's some sad shit. So you want to walk me home?

ARNIE

Yeah, I do.

GINA

Can you fuck?

ARNIE

I'm not sure.

GINA

Listen, I'm a genius, the highest IQ in the whole fucking school. I'm going to be a research doctor, cure all the crap we die from. Before we cut him open I volunteered to stick my finger up his dead ass and feel the killer gland, he was younger than you if that gives you any comfort, better looking too. When I cut it open I could see what kills men.

GINA, continued

It had a personality, the prostate cancer did. Like this thing I could have a conversation with, this growth. It was sort of like a flower. That's why I love men, this flower behind their balls, that kills them. The true poetry of life, of men. Then I cut off his cock, I mean he was dead, it was part of the autopsy, I sliced it like a banana and saw all the details of the motivation of the human male, the piss canal, the come canal. Do you still like me?

ARNIE

Yes, I like you a lot. Go on.

GINA

So I have this cock in my hand, this dead cock, off this dead body, and I want to cry, I put it in a little silver tray. Then we open his chest cavity and it's nothing, yes the heart and lungs, for some reason it had no interest for me, it wasn't the center. I want to meet death too, fucking head on, me and it. You know what I mean?

ARNIE

Yes, I know.

GINA

I'm into studying death. It blows me away, death. It's like here's this piece of music, it could be rap or Bach or some cornball love song, then it's over, then nothing, a memory, like you can sort of remember it, then it fades for the people who heard it, but it was there, for a space of time. Like this guy we cut up today. Nothing but meat, like if I cut you up, alive, it would be completely different. I want to understand that difference, that change, the switch. One day I'll be on that table and these students will be cutting me up, liver, brain, heart, reproductive system, cunt, ovaries, asshole…

ARNIE

That's not really reproductive, the anal cavity.

GINA

Really? You might be right, who knows?

ARNIE

Listen, what's your name?

GINA

Gina.

ARNIE

Yeah, Gina. Is it possible that I could write in my will that you cut me up when I die, you're the one that sees what's in there? Do the autopsy, the idea makes me sort of excited.

GINA

Well, tell me your name again.

ARNIE

Arnie, stupid name.

GINA

It's okay, like aren't we nice, Arn-nie. Aren't we nice.

ARNIE

Let's say you invite me up and we get all hot, take a shower, start to kiss, then we make love, have sex, what do you like to call it?

GINA

Fuck.

ARNIE

Yeah, fuck, and let's say I have a heart attack while we're fucking because I'm so out of control excited, my heart is pounding so hard.

GINA

Because all the blood is flowing down into your cock, out of your heart…

ARNIE

Yeah, nice, exactly. The question is; would you legally be able to cut me up, do the autopsy right there, like in your bathtub.

GINA
Legally, no. But would I do it, that's the question, isn't it?

ARNIE
It is, would you do it? You'd be with me at the moment of death, I'm inside you, than come and gone. So would you check me out? My insides?

GINA
God, yes. But not in my bathtub. I'd call an ambulance and have them bring you to St. Luke's, then I'd take you apart. Nerve by nerve, bone by bone.

ARNIE
Da Vinci cut up stolen dead bodies to better study the human form, to become a better painter. To get it! They would have locked him up today, put him in the nut house.

GINA
He didn't get caught, too fucking smart.

ARNIE
So, Gina, can I come up to your room?

GINA
Do you want to?

ARNIE
Yes I do.

ARNIE
(Aside)
Now when she raised her hands, looking at her armpits and the black hairs, I had never been so excited. She wore this little white innocent top, a young woman and how much I was hoping to die in her arms. We got up to her place, it was all right. There had been a show at the Modern of intimate photos of death, she had the book. I sat on the couch, very expensive Italian leather for such a small place, I looked at the beautiful photographs while she went into the bathroom, I

ARNIE, continued

heard water running. She came out nude and wet covered in some kind of blackness, like black soap that wasn't rinsed off.

GINA

So my friend said you were a great teacher. Is that right?

ARNIE

I was, no more. How old are you, Gina?

GINA

Twenty-one, lots of fun. Thirty-three, looking to be free, forty-four, should have been a whore, fifty-five, life is jive, sixty-six, no more dicks, seventy-seven, off to heaven.

ARNIE

My mother, sixty-six, no more dicks, died in a hospital. I watched her, listened to her, crazy, screaming about the wrong towels on the wrong shelf. I was with her, she was screaming about the things that were important to her. The fucking religion of neatness and order. God!

GINA

You stay with me tonight, no promises, if you can fuck, great. If you die on me, that's fine. Just don't ever lie to me. That is a sin unforgivable. You get it?

ARNIE

I get it.

ARNIE
(Aside)

Well I didn't die on Gina, in the morning I walked her to St. Lukes hospital holding hands, sun shining. She snuck me into the autopsy room, gave me a mask and a gown. There was a beautiful dead young Spanish woman on a clean table. I watched as Gina and the students and teacher opened her and cut her apart like a chicken.

I was surprised at the beauty, the lack of feelings, lack of blood, the

ARNIE, continued

stillness of the corpse. All of us masked like Batman or the Lone Ranger, looking for answers. It was nothing, meat. There was some whimpering from the young students and odor, indescribable, reminding me of my aging mother in the nursing home. The hardest thing was when they removed her dark eyeballs and opened her beautiful face. They put the parts in this metal tray to be studied further, closer. Cause of death: drug overdose.

I snuck a look at the papers. Maria Cortez, twenty-six. It was all so quiet, silent, except for the voice of the older doctor, a deep gentle voice, describing the body parts, like a soft piece of poetry. Maria Cortez, drug overdose. It took about two hours. No papers for organ donations. Maria's parts would be incinerated, turned into smoke, back to the sky. Gina's eyes turned to me once, when they removed Maria's eyes. I thought I saw a tear of compassion but maybe not. I felt a tear in my eyes, for Maria. Eyeless Goddess. The drug was heroin mixed with speed, cut with rat poison. Poor beautiful Maria. She only had a few tracks on her arm, one on her neck, like she was new at this. Gina said as she removed my smock and mask, I'll see you at the West End Bar at five o'clock, in a whisper in my ear.

GINA

So Arnie, what do you think?

ARNIE

The autopsy?

GINA

Yes.

ARNIE

Maria.

GINA

What do you think?

ARNIE

I think Maria was beautiful, Joan of Arc, till you took out her eyes, then I was frightened.

GINA
How do you mean?

ARNIE
Like we would all be struck dead for touching something sacred.

GINA
The eyes.

ARNIE
Yes, the eyes.

GINA
You want another beer?

ARNIE
No, something stronger. I feel like crying.

GINA
Like a bourbon.

ARNIE
I mean, she was so beautiful.

GINA
She's over and gone, done with. Headed for cremation.

ARNIE
You do this every day?

GINA
Every day, cutting up the dead.

ARNIE
That's why the armor.

GINA
I guess so.

ARNIE

You're so hot.

GINA

See, I love that, putting that piece together, the death cadence. I got hot cutting up her piece of ass body, I felt a tingle in my cunt and my heart and my mind, I know that's so bad. But fuck, I'm alive and feelings are feelings. The hair on her legs, the clean ears and lungs, the bush between her legs. I don't want to waste it. We're friends, right?

ARNIE

Right.

GINA

Soon I'll be a doctor, but I want to get it, the transformation, I need to get it. Do you need to get it?

ARNIE

I am on to something. I swear, we're a good team, you and I.

ARNIE
(Aside)

Now this is love, Gina and I. But she has me and this young boyfriend who she makes love to while I'm in her apartment. I have to wait in the bathroom while she does him. He's this cool black guy named Rashid, after he's done and leaves she's all tearful and wants to hold me, he does her real hard, I hear her screams. Then I lay next to her, my body pressed against her beautiful ass, and I hold her against me. She's all broken up, tearful and shit. So I hold her and we sleep. I say: Gina, I love you. She says, go to sleep, lover boy. Find your transition. Then she says:

GINA

I'm with you because, I want to be with you when you die, here in my bed. You are so close, it's so beautiful. The exit, the end.

ARNIE
(Aside)

Now I want to die for her, I mean I'm gone, in love. Spinning in the

ARNIE, continued

heat. She does me up and down, I feel the fade, the lights going out, a little cool pain in my head. Her on top of me, tits flying.

Then Gina had a few weeks off and went on trip someplace. She said I couldn't stay in her place. I hang out in the cathedral when I can, sometimes in Riverside Park. I miss Judy, in the emptiness. So much time alone, watching the river.

JUDY

(Aside)

To tell you the truth, when he left, it was like a weight off me. I was worried about him, but not really very much. It was like I could breathe, for the first time in a long time. It was like this crazed freedom. I stayed home for months. I went to work and came home to the apartment, watched TV for a few weeks, then got books out of the library, novels and got into reading, it was this summer of reading.

Then I got horny, horny bad, this feeling. I bought a vibrator in a health food store, a massager. Then, God, I was embarrassed. One night I had a few drinks and went into a video store and rented some porno movies. I was crazed watching them. I couldn't believe what these women did, I watched their faces, it seemed real, and the men, so hard and big and erect, I didn't want to be turned on but I was. When the men were about to come and pulled out and touched themselves and came, ejaculated on the women's breasts or faces, I mean there was no lie in that, in their orgasms. It made me hot, I'd put the vibrator on myself and feel so complete. I was embarrassed at how good it felt. And the women so beautiful. I wondered — what does it take for a woman that beautiful, so perfect, to do that, for a camera, for money. I watched over and over again. I had a million orgasms, with no guilt or pay back. I did it in the morning and when I came home from work and when I went to bed. It was so simple, so easy, so good. I loved to see the new cocks, the men exposed, it looked like pain on their faces when they came, that part made me sad, but I didn't want to see them smile. It made me all wet and crazed, but I never wanted be touched. The vibrator made it so easy to come, watching the men jerk off on the beautiful women's faces. I did not want any human contact. I saw my body in the full-length mirror, after the coming, I saw I was not like the women in the movies, but hotter and more real. I did not want a man or anyone. I wanted myself.

ARNIE
(Aside)
I miss Judy bad, really bad. But I know if I try to make any contact it will just be one more reason to blow my brains out. I walked into Bellevue and walked out. I couldn't really do it, put myself away. I know what they do and how they would destroy my soul, medicate it. It's true I have these terrible thoughts of rape, crime, to get the big payback.

The thought of making fifty grand on the Wheel, and waiting outside of Judy's apartment house in a nice new car. In a nice new suit. Sinatra on the stereo, "I've got you under my skin."

Can you imagine how Sinatra felt, singing those tunes in front of a big band, Jesus that must feel great, singing in front of the Basie Band, man that must feel good, really fucking good, the best. In a tux and all, man that's something, that must be some feeling, in Vegas, with all his buddies, fuck! And he, Sinatra was all depressed when Ava Gardner rejected him. Jesus! He could have all the women in the world, but the one he wanted he couldn't have, that's really something.

JUDY
(Aside)
I do miss him. Not his insanity. When he goes off, he's very angry. I'm not sure what that anger is about. I get angry about small things close to me. When it's hot and the air conditioner doesn't work, when I'm in the shower and forgot to buy soap, when I just miss a train or can't get a cab. But I don't hate the world the way he does. I know the small things will go away. But the way he's angry at the world, the people in it, it becomes boring, dull. Interesting how passion and hate can become dull. How passion becomes something I want to run from. I have friends, I like to laugh. My fear is that I can't escape him, that one day he'll try to kill me. I mean I see these TV shows about how crazy men get. I know he's capable of that. I'm very afraid of Arnold, as much as I used to love him, he works in a strange way, the way his mind works is abnormal. Dangerous. I do not want live in his world.

ARNIE
(Aside)
Today I was forced to go to the doctor. I'm in Hillside Hospital out

ARNIE, continued

in Queens, yes because I don't want to lose Judy, I'm in this fucking place. So this fucking doctor says:

DOCTOR

Arnold, I've got some bad news, you've got lung cancer, we're going to move you to Long Island Jewish hospital, to treat you for cancer.

ARNIE

Yeah, well I think all doctors are pricks.

DOCTOR

I understand you're emotionally disturbed, but this is medical, do you understand, there's cancer in your lungs.

ARNIE

I get it, cancer in my lungs. So I'm dying, is that what you're saying?

DOCTOR

No, you're going for treatment, it's advanced, yes, but I can't say you're dying. Radiation does amazing things. So, Thursday a van is going to take you to Long Island Jewish, to treat your cancer.

ARNIE
(*Aside*)

So they take me off in this fucking ugly Blue Plymouth Van, this shit hole van to treat me, funny word "treat", a fucking Halloween word, treat. I have this nice conversation with the driver before I tell him he's a stupid dick for driving helpless people around.

ARNIE

You're a dumb fat motherfucker with an ugly fat neck.

VAN DRIVER

At least I'm not nuts like you, motherfucker.

ARNIE

They told me I have cancer. You ever have cancer?

VAN DRIVER

No.

ARNIE

I can't hear you.

VAN DRIVER

No, I've never had cancer.

ARNIE

Well I think they're full of shit and I can prove it.

VAN DRIVER

Why don't you just shut up and let me drive you to your treatment?

ARNIE

How'd you get so fat, eating chips and jerking off? Stuffing yourself with crap, watching TV, getting hypnotized, that crap will kill you, stupid motherfucker. Asshole van driver.

VAN DRIVER

Listen pal, I make my fucking living, okay, now shut the fuck up and let me do my job.

ARNIE

You live my life, that's a fucking job. That's work with no pay. Crap job.

VAN DRIVER

Poor baby.

ARNIE
(Aside)

Now this big ass guy stops at a light and I book, jump out of the fucking van and run down into the subway station. Fuck lung cancer, I'm really pissed off.
I don't have a fucking thing except these clothes I'm wearing, dick van driver. Why do I hate everything? Not because of lung cancer, it

ARNIE, continued
doesn't even hurt. I don't give a shit about dying. I think it might be the perfect state of being, not being.
I think I'm pissed because I never got to sing those songs in front of a big swinging, burning band. Just have a perfect moment, a moment of perfection, where all the phrasing fits. I can't even imagine how that feels. And he was in pain because Ava Gardner didn't love him, Jesus Frank, I get it. Judy doesn't love me. Do you think my pain is anything like yours? I mean here I am in Coney Island, in hospital clothes, no tux, no nothing. I can't cry either. Frank, what do you think? Is my pain like yours? I know you're dead, I don't like it that you're dead. What do you think?

FRANK
It was pretty bad, sure I was famous, like you said, I had lots of women and money and had this talent, my voice, but I felt bad. I don't know where it came from, my ability to sing a song, I never thought it was that important, except it felt so good, in my throat. I don't know why Ava didn't love me, I would have done anything for her.

ARNIE
Would you have given up singing, not made those records with Nelson Riddle, I mean they were genius, perfect. Would you have given that up for Ava?

FRANK
It never came up, and no, I would not. No, I would not. You know why?

ARNIE
God's gift, you can't turn your back on that shit.

FRANK
Exactly right.

ARNIE
See Frank, I have no gift like you. God, I wish I did. That must feel so good. I don't have that. I can't imagine having that, so I feel like less,

ARNIE, continued

no, I am less. I had all your records, man, you were so perfect. Really some hot shit. Plus being a movie star and having your pals, Dean and Sammy, hanging out with JFK and Marilyn and…

FRANK

Arnie, we're all human beings, I had a gift and luck and ambition. I'm dead Arnold, and you're alive. I got fat and old and couldn't nail the notes.

ARNIE

Frank, you were never fat. They loved you.

FRANK

I got heavy, okay and yeah they applauded, for the memory of what I was. I heard it and I know they did too, but they clapped anyway, for the memory. Don't you think that hurt? All of us knowing it, in Madison Square Garden where I saw Joe Louis, the Brown Bomber, fight. I sounded bad. Sure I got a few million, and I smiled, an old man. I could hear when notes were out of tune or when my voice gave out, you want to talk about pain, and they smiled and clapped and everyone kissed my ass. I knew it, they knew it.
"New York, New York", I hate that song, I couldn't sing it and they went nuts. But I knew the truth and they had to know it too. It was all a fucking game. I should have never done it.

ARNIE

But Frank…

FRANK

Don't do it, I have no news for you. I'm dead, you're alive. Deal with it.

ARNIE

But Frank…

FRANK

Listen, when Sammy died and Dean died, I wondered what this fucking world is about. Dean was a talent, really he could sing, and act, he

FRANK, continued

had a good heart and was so handsome. Everyone thought without Jerry he was nothing, he proved them wrong and he was a pal. You have any pals, Arnie?

ARNIE

Nobody. Listen Frank, I'm so honored to…

FRANK

Sammy, no one like him, a little black kid who could sing and dance his ass off, do great impersonations. Lost an eye in a car crash, and persevered, became a Jew. I loved Sammy, what a talent. We were nothing, no George Washington or Einstein, nothing, entertainers. Singers, actors, big deal. Without the songwriters I could have never done it, Cole Porter, Jerome Kern, Gershwin…

ARNIE

But Frank…

FRANK

But nothing.

ARNIE

But Frank…

FRANK

Nothing…

ARNIE

But Frank…

FRANK

Not Beethoven, or Bach, a cool singer, big deal.

ARNIE

Hey, you are Frank Sinatra.

FRANK

Was…

ARNIE

Frank Sinatra, that is something, compared to me. You have great records that people still listen to. They love those records. They'll love them till there's no humanity left. They'll hear that shit on some planet in some other solar system when we burn up or freeze up and be blown away. Jesus, Frank. So Frank, do you think that was God given, the talent?

FRANK

Luck, pal. Luck and hard work. I had to learn the songs, it didn't come out of the air. Every word of every song and find some meaning in those words. Yeah the phrasing came easy. Find the notes. I really don't know were God comes in. I had something I could do, so I did it.

ARNIE

But did you ever have doubt about yourself?

FRANK

No, never. My ability to sing, no. Making those movies with Gene Kelly, dancing and shit, I doubted a lot of things. That was work, bullshit work. But it paid a lot of money and gave me more exposure.

ARNIE

So you're good now.

FRANK

No, I'm not good, I'm dead. Alone. It's not some big jazz movie heaven, it's nothing, nothing. I'm not hanging with Dean or Sammy or Basie, my wife or dogs. Nothing.

ARNIE

(*Aside*)

Then he was gone, nothing. Now I'm on this other subway platform, West Fourth Street, there's a huge poster across the platform that says, "Treatment Works". I figure nothing works. I am sure I'm not insane, I am sure I'm on to something. I can hear Frank singing; "I've got you under my skin", I know if I just sit here long enough, everyone will either pass or get off one of these trains.

ARNIE, continued

My father: Make something of yourself. Work hard, make a life for yourself.
My mother: You're a good boy, grow up and study, I love you.
Then Judy gets off the D train. It must be morning. Her hair is all long and down, she's wearing a camel's hair coat. She's with a man with neatly combed dark blond hair, well dressed, standing tall, they hold hands and seem to be talking in slow motion.

ARNIE

Judy! Judy!

ARNIE
(Aside)
The man comes close to me, he stinks from aftershave lotion.

MAN

Don't stalk, Arnie, she's done with you. Don't wait for her or call her. It's over. I'll break your neck if you ever try to get near her again.

ARNIE

I was just…

MAN

Do you understand, we'll have you arrested, do you get that, stay away. Stay away from Judy and me. You're a fucking sick bum. Stay away, you get that?

ARNIE

I'm just sitting, waiting.

MAN

Just stay away. It's over!

ARNIE

Judy!

ARNIE
(Aside)
The guy just slams me against the bench, I feel it on my back. A hard slam, Judy just looks away. Like I don't exist. Judy's head is down, he has me by the throat.

MAN
Fucking stay away from her, you got that pal?

ARNIE
(Aside)
It was the "Pal" that got me. I got up and pushed him right into the oncoming "E" train. The train hit him hard, he flew like an ugly overgroomed bird. Judy ran, disappeared.
I sat back down on my bench. Waiting, wondering at the wonder. Did it really happen or was it just in my head, my mind? There's no corpse, no crowd, no police in this ugly tiled tunnel, like a tubular shower. Fuck I'm not sure, maybe it's the drugs they gave me in the hospital wearing off.
I sit there and hope for my med student to appear, Gina. I see her opening my chest, my lungs and finding these pockets of growths, like little hard beautiful marbles, little pearls, to make a bracelet or necklace, filling the tiny lung sacks like an internal garden, seeds for some other life, some new living thing, to be planted in a new kind of garden. Then I find her on Upper Broadway.

ARNIE
Gina, I looked for you, waited for you, please don't leave.

GINA
It's hopeless. That's what I figure, it's hopeless. I don't want to be a goddamn doctor. Arnie, you know what's there, nothing, meat, meat and tangles. Like a steak dinner. A crummy piece of meat. Like taking apart a radio, expecting to find the music inside the radio.

ARNIE
I know Gina, I know, that's what I'm working on, day and night, that's what I work on.

GINA

I know you do. It's troubling, isn't it?

ARNIE

It's the worst kind of trouble. Gina, where have you been? What's wrong, Gina, where did you go on your vacation?

GINA

I went to Spanish Harlem, I saw Rashid's wife shoot him, she almost got me. He was on top of me, the bullet went through his back and something in his chest, his heart, stopped the bullet from going through both of us. The look on her face, it's captured here in my head forever, she just stared at me, our eyes met for what seemed like forever. You know like those still frames in a movie. His weight on top of me just changed, like, first heavy, then light. And these two black kids were just looking, just looking. Beautiful kids. The three of them walked out, didn't turn back, his blood, warm, bathing me, I could feel him getting soft inside me. Then I just walked out. Got a gypsy cab and came home. That was my vacation. Rashid is dead!

ARNIE

I'm sorry, Jesus…Did you love him?

GINA

No.

ARNIE

You ever been in love?

GINA

Never, never even close.

ARNIE

You ever want a house in the country, filled with kids and dogs and a vegetable garden? To hold someone close who you cared about, every night to hold someone close, make love some nights, some nights just be together and talk about bullshit, the car, the garden, the bank account, winter clothes. That kind of shit. You ever want that?

GINA
No, never.

ARNIE
I'm sorry Gina. See, I wanted that, I did. To never have outside needs. To make a self-contained world that nothing could penetrate or interfere with. God, did I want that.

GINA
Arnie my heart goes out to you, that's some sad corny shit. It doesn't exist, it's a dream. A corny dream. From some crap TV shows that you grew up with, Desi and Lucy, Ralph and Alice, Father Knows Best. The Brady Bunch. A dream, an American dream.

ARNIE
Gina, GINA! I have cancer. (*Pause*) Let's say I told you I love you, let's say that. If you're a doctor or a floor sweep, no matter what.

GINA
I'd say you're too old for me, too poor for me, too crazy for me, someone who's a failure, interesting but not exciting or handsome enough. So I'd never be that girl of your dreams, so I'd reject your love flat out. Will I screw you tonight? I might, I might not. If I don't get a better offer, yes, sure, I'd rather not be alone with my thoughts. I like your company.

ARNIE
That's something, that is something. I think you're becoming a little hard, you know, tough. Maybe you spend too much time digging around inside corpses. Gina, maybe you should call your family, your mom and dad, maybe you should go home for awhile. Where are they? Gina, where are your parents?

GINA
My parents! My parents are on dad's yacht somewhere, off the coast of Spain or it could be Rio or the Grenadines, sipping Martinis, entertaining good-looking people. Having fun. Listening to string quartets. They're so fucking complacent, always making things beautiful,

GINA, continued

perfect. The word that describes them is elegant. Fucking elegant. They never worked a day in their lives, either one of them. They are beyond rich, all handed to them. Why are you asking me all this shit?

ARNIE

I just am, I don't know.

GINA

You'd like my mother. As a matter of fact she might like you, think you're eccentric and interesting. She's so damn beautiful, always in Paris-white, dark hair, dark tanned smooth skin, black eyes, perfect body. Fresh vegetables, fresh fruit and fresh fish. That's her answer to everything. Fresh vegetables, fresh fruit and fresh fish. They have a goddamn garden on the boat!

ARNIE

Really?

GINA

Yeah. A fucking vegetable garden on a boat. They don't fucking get it.

ARNIE

Don't get what?

GINA

That it's ugly and painful, inside those bodies, it's ugly. Filled with unwanted growths and poison, it's a fucking war, there is a war inside every one of us. If you eat fresh everything or shoot junk, it's a world class war, it doesn't care. It has no plot because death always, always wins, it always wins. Always. That's what they don't get and can't handle. I cut up a woman the other day who had a baby spoon inside her stomach. A baby spoon that gave her a life of pain. On the handle it said "Sterling". It was engraved, "Eva we love you forever." And it killed her, caused her terrible pain. You're distracting me from picking up other guys. You're being clever by asking me about myself. Are you being clever, Arnie?

ARNIE

No.

GINA

Sure you are, the survival instinct. The survival gimmick. You play a good game, faking interest in me and covering up your terrible need. Do you want to hold a living, breathing human body, the giant hot water bottle of caring? Tough, isn't it?

ARNIE

It's tough all right.

GINA

I'm going to fix you up with my mother; you'd like her better than me. You can talk your philosophy, she'd be fascinated, interested, and you can make love to her while dad is at the helm. You're part of their world, not mine. Would you like that, Arnie?

ARNIE

I'm not sure.

GINA

I'm sure.

(*Gina takes out cell phone*)

Yes daddy, I'm fine…all A's, the top of the top of my class…I do like it…Listen Daddy I met this terrific philosophy professor here at school, who has a vacation coming up. He loves sailing, you know teacher's pay…He's a wonderful man, you'd really enjoy his company…Yes, Virgin Gorda in two days, the British Virgins…on the card…that's very generous Daddy. Put mom on, oh she's on the speaker phone…Mom, you'll love him, eccentric, interesting, he needs a sailing vacation badly…well he's not bad, nice looking man, he could use a little sun and fresh fish…yes and vegetables…yes and fruit! Jesus!…of course he is…very bright…the marina in Virgin Gorda, Thursday afternoon…Dr. Arnold Gold…Yes at the airport…love you too…it's okay, you don't have to be here for my graduation, I understand, they're so boring, graduations…I don't really need a car in New York, but thanks anyway…He'll be there. I love you too…Maybe next summer…I will try…Take care…Ciao to you too.

(*Off phone*)

Ciao, Arnold.

ARNIE
(Aside)

So there it was, Gina bought me some clothes and gave me money for a cab to Kennedy and a bottle of Valium for the flight. My ticket waiting for me at Kennedy. Puerto Rico, then a one-engine, ten seater to Virgin Gorda, and there was a car to meet me. A smiling black man holding a sign. "Doctor Gold." It was dusk, the sun setting, then to the marina. There they were, perfect, handsome, both of them. Robert and Susan, just as Gina had described them, elegant. Susan and Robert, all smiles. They shake hands with me and say: "Welcome to paradise".

I could feel the electricity. We had cocktails on the boat, Goddess of the Seas, silver letters across her stern.

We talked about art, music, belief systems, I made a good show of myself. They made me so comfortable, all elegance, intelligence and beauty. I slept soundly, Susan came and gave me a sweet kiss goodnight. In the morning, off we sailed, after a breakfast of lobster meat, fresh corn and Jamaican coffee. It's a sixty-five foot schooner, black hull, red sails, she is a Goddess. A beautiful blonde woman cook from Norway trained in Paris. Two huge black homosexuals from Rio crewing. Robert is a handsome white haired man who scuba dives for fish each day and spends the rest of his time reading from their wonderful onboard library. Five o'clock are cocktails and conversation, then dinner.

When there's no land in sight, time stops, there is no time. At night, under the milky way, there's string quartet music, Bach and later Bartok. I'm sure I died and went to the perfect place.

Somewhere back in the ugly man-made city, Gina is dissecting my remains and Judy eats them cooked in fresh garlic and olive oil. I sit on the bow and watch the water pass. I'm good. Lucky. We're headed for Barbados, then Greece. I'm good, I think.

In my berth at night I feel safe, the movement on the sea, the rocking and tilt, afloat on the huge mother sea.

ARNIE, continued

I beat Robert at chess tonight after several cognacs, under the full moon, so I guess my mind still works. When I moved the rook to checkmate Robert, I didn't recognize my hands or my tanned fingers. I'm on board.

JUDY
(Aside)

I got a card from Greece, from Arnold, imagine Greece, a picture of the Acropolis; "Dear Judy, I'm sorry it didn't work out with us. I got stuck, run aground, confused. I tied my own tangled knot, not aware that I was including you, that was needy and selfish. I've learned how to tie knots and, more important, how to untie them. Have a good life. Arnold."

My life is good, I met a man who works in my office, he takes me to lunch and sometimes dinner. We go to baseball games, the Mets and the Yankees, he's not as good at the Wheel as Arnie was, and doesn't go crazy for Vanna. He bought me this state of the art hot air popcorn maker. He's very sweet and kind of handsome. He makes no demands on me. We're starting to plan our marriage. I'm comfortable with him, that's all I ever wanted. Comfort and safety.

GINA
(Aside)

I'm glad I could do something for him, something unselfish, the first unselfish thing I've done in a long time, maybe he taught me something. He's a bright man, just made a wrong turn somewhere and couldn't get back.

It happens, it could happen to you or me, any of us. He sent me this card; "Dear Gina, Athens is so beautiful. I'm becoming a good sailor, tying knots and everything, your dad lets me take the helm, night watch, under the stars and moon, while they sleep below. Something has changed, everything has changed. Thank you, dear Gina. When you take a break from looking into corpses, take a night sail and check out the sky. It changes it all. Love, Arnie."

I'm an intern now, two weeks in maternity, watching births, delivering

GINA, continued

babies, taking care of preemies, little babies, putting my finger in their tiny hands, rubbing their tiny feet and toes. How they fight for every breath, to be part of this world, this existence, not knowing why. It's really something. Really something.

END OF PLAY

KONG WASH

Kong Wash 2001

First Production, Club Metronome
Burlington, VT
Directed by the author

Original Cast

Kong – Jordan Gullikson
Kara – Sue Ball
Pig – Aaron Masi
Dot – Cherry Tart
Babe – Pamela Formica
Cabbie – Paul Soychak
Nancy – Emer Pond Feeney
Mrs. Epstein – Cherry Tart
Announcer – Peter Freyne
Judge – Peter Freyne
Man – Peter Freyne

Cast of Characters

Kong (Russ) – Wrestler
Pig (Paulie) – Kong's younger brother
Kara – Kong's Wife
Dot – Woman card player
Babe – Woman card player
Cabbie – Russian cab driver
Mrs. Epstein – Old Woman
Nancy – Young Girl
Announcer – Voice
Judge – Voice

Kong Wash

ACT I
Scene 1

*(Women playing cards, Stage Left.
Kong working out in full wrestling costume, Stage Right.)*

KARA
So Dottie, how was Disneyland or was it Disneyworld?

DOT
World, land, who the hell knows. The kids loved it, I tell you when little Bobby saw fuckin' Mickey Mouse I thought he was gonna go nuts, his face, Jesus, you should have seen it. You want to see the pictures?

KARA
Yeah but after we're done playing. You want to deal?

DOT
Let Babe deal. Tommy was pissed the whole time.

BABE
You deal, Kara.

KARA
No, you deal. What does a grown man want to see Mickey Mouse for?

DOT
He couldn't wait to get home.

BABE
Robby refused to go to Disneyland, we won a free trip.

KARA

No shit.

BABE

Yeah, shit Kara, I told you last year, the Kix box top thing, we won. Robby tried to get the money instead of the trip, but we had to go. In the end it cost us three hundred bucks, I thought he was gonna kill me. He spent the whole time at the bar.

KARA

Kong hates that shit too. He won't even go to playland at Burger King. The kids love it. Watch this.(*Yelling*) HEY KONG, YOU WANT TO TAKE THE KIDS TO BURGER KING?

KONG

SHUT UP, KARA. I HATE THAT FUCKIN' PLACE !

(*Women laughing*)

KARA

They hate that shit.

DOT

I'm walking around in my little cut off jeans and halter top, so Goofy comes over, you know joking with the kids. And Tommy says, Goofy has a hard-on for me, like he's gonna punch him out. I tell him it's part of the costume. So Tommy tells him to fuck off. He actually says, "Goofy, fuck off."

BABE

So does he?

DOT

Fuckin' Goofy is gone like the wind. I think he did have a hard-on.

BABE

Hey Kara, why's Kong working out up here?

KARA

The basement's all fucked up, we had to call Roto Rooter, the sewer backed up, it's a fuckin' mess down there. He's got a big match tomorrow. He's got to be pumped. HEY KONG!

KONG

WHAT!

KARA

WOULD YOU GET ME AND THE LADIES SOME MORE CHIPS?

KONG

I'M WORKING MY TRICEPS, DON'T FUCK WITH ME, KARA!

KARA

IF YOU LOVE ME, THEN YOU'LL GET THEM.

DOT

Jesus Kara.

KARA

Watch. PLEASE HONEY, WE'RE IN THE MIDDLE OF A HAND. PLEASE, HONEY.

KONG

FUCK! (KONG drops his weight and brings over a bag of chips.) Kara.

KARA

Yeah, honey.

KONG

Don't ever interrupt my workout.

KARA

Thank you, Kong. (*Gives him a little kiss*) Who's my good boy.

KONG

Jesus, Kara.

                           BABE
Kong.

                           KONG
What!

                           BABE
You're lookin' good.

                           KONG
Yeah.

                           KARA
I love you, honey.

                           KONG
Yeah.

                           DOT
Hey Kong, me and Tommy are goin' to your match tomorrow.

                           KONG
Yeah, that's great.
             (*KONG goes back to working out.*)

                           DOT
You goin', Kara?

                           KARA
I can't watch that shit, I mean I watch it on TV. When it looks like he's getting hurt I can turn it off.

                           DOT
What are you playin'?

                           KARA
Jacks!

DOT
Really.

BABE
What is she playing?

KARA
Jacks.

(*KONG bicep pump with weight, tape measure on bicep.*)

KONG
Fuck yeah!

DOT
So, years ago, I met this guy in Spain, he said he was a teacher. English you know, from England, nasal.

KARA
Nasal.

DOT
Yeah, like the lips move but the sound comes through the nose.

BABE
(*Nasal, holding nose, fake English accent, kidding around*)
Darling, a spot of tea or a spotting on your undies, I've been spotting terribly, it's that time darling, the time of the spot, the spotting time.

DOT
(*English accent*)
Oh Noel, darling, will you get me a truffle?

KARA
You have cards, honey?

DOT
I have cards.

KARA

Deal, just deal.

DOT

Up or down?

KARA

I really don't care.

BABE

You must care, caring is everything, without caring there is no winning. without winning there's no caring.

DOT

Always losing creates a lack of caring, so winning, if it occurs, becomes a meaningless situation, all the rules are changed.

KARA

Hit me, either way, as long as I'm hit.

PIG
(*Off stage voice*)

You let me out of here, fuckers, let me out, I never hurt anybody. Who did I hurt, name my hurt. Stupid motherfuckers, who, name them.

JUDGE
(*Voice off stage*)

Your mother, your sisters, your father, your children, your brother, your grand and great grandparents on all sides. I sentence you to death. I want you to see yourself, in a bad way, in lethal rope.

KARA

This guy I met, before Kong, a real famous comic. He was stupid and drunk and fat. So I'm tryin' to think. I mean, how can I capitalize on this to make money, I never did. I reflected on that, I did, he was a pretty sad guy. So I'm thinkin', I use people.

DOT

I never had sex with anyone famous. I've had some studs and...

PIG
(*Banging and ringing at door*)

Hey, hey, big brother, open up, come on, Russ, I need some help, open up, I know you're in there. Hey man, open the fuckin' door. I seen you on TV, fucker. Your jive car's here, the Kongmobile, you're in there. I'll smash the fuckin' windshield, I'll wake up the whole fuckin' middle class neighborhood. Open up King Kong, it's your brother.

(*KONG comes to the door, opens it and smashes PIG a good one to the head.*)

PIG

Oh man, oh man.

KONG

What do you want?

PIG

I just...

KONG

I told you to stay away from me. Did I tell you that? Did I?

PIG

Yeah, yeah, yeah. Help me out, okay...

KONG

How'd you get out here?

PIG

I took a cab, and I fuckin' jumped out at the avenue. He's probably lookin' for me, the cabbie, circling around, please man let me in, it was over twenty-five bucks, lower east side to Rockaway. These guys were after me, I didn't know where else to go. Please Russ, please just this once, I'll leave in the morning.

KONG

Listen Pig shit, I don't want you here.

PIG
You don't understand, these guys are gonna kill me, till morning, then I'm gone, I'll sleep in the garage. I won't bother anyone, then I'm gone.

KONG
Listen prick, I have a big match tomorrow and Kara has friends over for a card game. I need my rest, I'm wrestling at the fuckin' Nassau Coliseum, I need to concentrate, plan my moves.

PIG
I know, I know, please man, there's the cabbie, they'll bust me again. I go back to the joint once more, I'll die. Please, I'll crash and leave in the morning. Please, Kong, I fuckin'…

KONG
You sleep in the car, the Buick, in the garage.

PIG
Thanks man, you're a good guy. Kong, could I get some food?
   (*Walks around women's card game, grabs some potato chips.*)

KONG
Put those down.

PIG
Sorry man. What are you ladies playing?

BABE
Black card slut stud, it's a game we invented on the beach.

PIG
What's the rules?

DOT
The sentence goes: What are the rules, not "What's the rules."

KARA
Ladies, this is my brother-in-law, Paulie, we call him Pig.

PIG
So, can I play?

KARA
Take a walk, Pig.

KONG
Get away from them, I'll break you in half. I have to concentrate. I'm fighting Rhino tomorrow. So fuck off!

PIG
Come on man, (*joking*) come on punk, I'll smash you in half.

BABE
You guys shut up, can't you see we're playing a game. Jesus Christ!

PIG
(*Taking KONG aside*)
Listen, I'm not in good shape, okay. I lost my place, I have no money, I jumped out of a cab and the guy is circling, the meter was up there, twenty or thirty bucks. The whole time I'm freaked because I know I'm gonna jump, I get in this conversation with the driver about sitcoms, situation comedies, the guy is weird, from Russia or someplace, I'm trying to tell him how the laughter is all canned and he's telling me about how he's gonna save his family and save his money and get them over here, to America, how he studied the New York map, how he can find anyplace in any borough.

He doesn't know what I'm talking about, canned laughter, and I don't get Russia or the Soviet Union, the green card shit. And like I'm thinking, this guy is hungry and I'm hungry, and I'm thinking this guy never did crack, because then the only thing he would care about is crack, it would solidify all his hopes and problems, I mean in a physical nonromantic way. I have to admit the accent had this scary ring to it. Like some Nazi kind of shit, but I know the guy is just trying to make it, like he has some ideal that we don't have. The cool thing is I know I'm gonna jump out of the cab and run, beat the fare and he's all hot about making money in America, I'm thinking, I'll show you pal, about how America works, I mean keep your eyes

PIG, continued

open, cause we kick ass. Kong, do we kick ass? Look at this specimen, (*Referring to Kong*) is this a man or what! We should shut the lights off because this guy wants his money.

KONG

Well, you might just sleep in jail.

PIG

I need a shower, would that be okay? A shower and a sandwich. Any of you ladies want to shower with me, I look better wet. Hey come on, that's funny. Come on, cheer up.

KARA

Get him out of here, face down. Deal!

KONG

(*Taking PIG aside*)

Come here. Listen punk, I've got two kids sleeping, in their own rooms. I made this place, I fought for this life. They go to a nice school, they play musical instruments, they are good kids. Pig, I don't want you here, you get that? Look at me, I don't want you in my life, in my house, I'm sorry for you. But you're a pain the ass. You get that? You made your choices. I'm makin' it as a wrestler, and I don't owe you anything. You sleep in the car tonight and then go.

PIG

I need a bed, one night, I need to feel like a human being. One night between clean sheets, in a home, a home with kids, please Kong. It's bad.

KONG

My friend, brother. You don't know what bad is. I AM BAD. I am the villain, the loser, they kick Kong's ass, every time, for now I'm the bad guy, but I get five grand a match, to be hated. Do you get that? To get paid for being hated?

PIG

Yeah, well I get hated for free. Nothing, except what I steal.

KONG

Listen Pig…

PIG

Please don't call me that. Paulie, call me Paulie, please man.
(*Knocking on door*)
Oh man, it's the cabbie, please don't tell him I'm here, please, man.

KONG

I'm never lying for you again, you got that, you got that? I don't protect you!
(*KONG goes to the door*)

PIG

Please Russ, please man, please.

(*KONG goes to the door. CABBIE at the door*)

CABBIE
(*Russian accent*)
I saw him, lousy punk son-of-bitch, try to stiff me twenty-six dollars. He's in here, don't bullshit me. My country, he goes to Siberia for that shit.

KONG

Hey slugger, calm down or I'll send you to Siberia.

CABBIE

I want money for my work, fucking punk!

KONG

Hey! There's ladies here. Watch your mouth or you won't have one! PIG!

PIG

WHAT!

CABBIE

That's him. YOU PUNK!

PIG

I never seen him before.

KONG

PIG! Look at him, is this the guy you ripped off?

PIG

How do I know? I ripped off a lot of guys.

CABBIE

Listen mister I picked him up on Ninth Avenue, all the way to fucking Rockaway. Twenty-six bucks.

KONG

HEY! (*Picking him up by the throat*) You watch your mouth. PIG, is this the guy?

PIG

NO!

KARA

HEY! We're playing a game! Sorry ladies.

PIG

Sorry ladies!

CABBIE

You Americans think you own the world.

KONG

We do own the world. PIG!

PIG

"We are the world, (*Singing*) We are the children…"

KONG

Look at him Pig, look this man in the face.

PIG
Yeah so. I never seen his ugly face before.

CABBIE
You die in hell. Twenty-six bucks and no fare back.

KONG
(*Grabbing PIG in hammer lock*)
Is this the guy, the truth.

PIG
Yeah yeah okay, it's the Commie creep. Comes to our country to take our money son-of-a-bitch Commie bastard, prick face punk...

KONG
Shut it! KARA! Get me fifty bucks.

KARA
JESUS! Every time he comes around it costs us money.

KONG
Get it Kara!

KARA
Yeah, yeah...

PIG
Don't give him a lousy cent.

CABBIE
He jumped out on the avenue. I stop for a...

KONG
SHUT IT! (*Kara gives Kong the money, Kong hands it to PIG.*) Now pay the man...(*PIG tries to pocket some of the money*)...all of it.

PIG
Jesus, Kong, the guy can't even fuckin' drive.

KONG

Pay him!

PIG

Here you go, you fuckin' little alien. (*Pays him*)

CABBIE

Thanks, mister. (*PAUSE*) I saw you on TV. KONG! You're Kong, the wrestler.

KONG

You forget you were ever here. GO!

CABBIE

You sign my book, hey, you sign my book? I got Faye Dunaway, Robert De Niro, Clint Eastwood, Madonna, Charles Barkley…

KONG

GO!

(*Exit Cabbie*)

PIG

Thanks Russ, thanks.

KONG

Don't ever do this again, you fucking got that?

PIG

Yeah, yeah, thanks man. Really thanks. I didn't know where else…

KONG

I want you to get out of here. I don't care if you have to walk back to the city. You screwed up my workout. And you're screwing up the ladies' card game. We got a life here, Pig, and you're not in it.

PIG

Listen, Russ…

KONG

You call me Kong.

PIG

Yeah, yeah, what ever you want. I'm in trouble, "Kong", we're brothers right.

KONG

We're nothing.

PIG

We're brothers, no matter what you say you can't change that.

KONG

I can change whatever ever I want.

PIG

You're my big brother, that's blood man, you can't change that. I'd do anything for you.

KONG

Yeah, you want to go out and get slammed around for me, till you goddamn ache and can't move, huh pal, the Pig Man.

PIG

Russ, I mean Kong. (*Pause*) Rita's dead. My girl Rita's dead, I think she OD'd and they're lookin' for me…

KONG

You son-of-a bitch…

PIG

And there's a kid, a little kid, a baby, like three or four months old, she's with this old woman on Delancy Street, this old woman who's all screwed up on beer and amphetamine, and she takes like two hundred aspirin a day. She's got my kid, our kid, Rita and me. I didn't want to tell you, till we got it all together. We were gonna have this big party, and invite you and Kara, and show you the kid, all wrapped up like a Christmas present. We called her Nancy, after mom. If it was

PIG, continued

a boy we were gonna call him Kong, after you, man. "KONG", after you, my brother.

KONG

You're full of shit.

PIG

No man, Kong, it's true, I swear on dad's grave, it's true. Me and Rita, we partied, like we did before, a hundred times…

KONG

Drugs, fuckin dope, you're not makin any sense, you're confusing names and who's dead and who isn't…

PIG

Yeah, yeah but nothing we couldn't handle. We fall asleep and I wake up holding her and the kid and she's dead, ice cold dead. So I bring the kid to Mrs. Epstein, and took a cab here. Rita's dead. I was doing good, a messenger job, eight AM, I'm there delivering shit.

KONG

You have a job.

PIG

Shit, no, I mean yeah for a day or two. And I was dealing, just a little, on the side…So I called 911 from the street. I mean I covered her up and dressed her in these real nice black silk pajamas that she lifted from Bloomingdale's. She was the best, it was like touching a statue, a saint. She was the best in these classy department stores, just put the stuff on under her clothes, and bam, never got caught once, all class. She wasn't like me, she was all goodness. She would just steal beautiful things to look good for me. I swear to God. Please Kong, we got to get the kid, please man. I don't know where else to take her, except to you. She'll die with the old lady. Please, I'll never ask you anything again, I swear on mom's grave…

KONG

I need to talk to my wife. Kara!

KARA

Hey we got a game here, you get that Kong? We need to play on. Finish the hand.

PIG

Yeah kid, I mean Kong, I want us, now, tonight, to go get my daughter, Rita's daughter, and bring her back here to this nice house, so she can sleep in a house, a real house, with blood, with family, I'm scared man, she's gonna die too, just a little baby. Please Kong, help me, this once. I'll never ask you for anything again.

KONG

Watch little brother,. (*Lifting weights*) You see the veins in my arms, no emotion, power. Do you see that, power, pressure. You want me to drive you, us, into New York, to Delancy Street to get your child, and bring her back here, for my wife to take care of, when I have a match with Rhino tomorrow. You're nuts, no way.

PIG

Please, man. They're gonna think I killed her, Rita, Jesus, the love of my life. We had a party, for the baby, three-month birthday, we gave her mashed bananas. Yeah we got high, it was a bad idea, I know. Please lets go get the kid. Please man, I screwed up, I really did, I'm sorry, Russ, Kong, please.

KONG

Kara, come here! Kara!

KARA

We're playing a damn game!

KONG

You're not bullshitting me, if you are I'll fucking break you in half.

PIG

No man, it's your niece, three months old, a little girl, please man, she's with this old lady who's filled with aspirin. Nancy with the laughing face, that's the song we were listening to when we conceived. "Nancy with the Laughing Face", Sinatra, please man, do this one thing

PIG, continued

for me and I'll never ask you for anything again. This old lady can't take care of a kid, she can't, her hands are all deformed, arthritic. The woman's old, beer with aspirin, that shit rots your stomach, I lost Rita, I can't lose...

KONG

Shut up, just shut up. KARA, COME OVER HERE!

KARA

It's my hand, I'm dealing, you promised you wouldn't screw up ladies card night.

KONG

GET OVER HERE!

KARA

You promised.

PIG

Please man, don't get mad.

KONG

COME HERE. NOW!

KARA

Excuse me, ladies. (*She goes over to Kong and Pig*)

KONG

It seems my kid brother has an infant child, from his dead dope fiend girlfriend, our niece, named Nancy...

PIG

Nancy with the laughing face...

KONG

Shut up, Pig.

PIG
Yeah, yeah, okay. Please Kara…

KONG
We're gonna go downtown and get her. He's fucked up my workout. I can't let a kid die. What do you think, is that okay with you? Kara, answer me.

PIG
Thank you, God bless you, you won't be sorry, oh man, thank you.

KARA
He's playing with your head, like he always does. Don't go. He just wants more money for crack.

PIG
I don't do crack, I swear, I swear on mom and dad's life, my baby, me and Rita, is with this crazy old lady, the kid's gonna die, please Kara, it's all I got left. Her name is Nancy, I swear to God.

KARA
How many times has he called you with crummy stories, how many times, don't buy it, look at him, he's lying through his teeth. You want to go, go. You need a good night's sleep, before tomorrow's match. Rhino'll break your back, you got to know the moves, and…

PIG
Please, Kara…

KARA
And you've got to be rested, this punk is lying…

PIG
I swear, it's no lie, this is a beautiful little girl. (*Pause*) Okay screw it, screw you all, I walk, screw you all, you too, ladies, have a good card game. I don't believe you people. Look at me Kara, screw you, I am telling the damn truth. You make me sick, all of you.

KONG

What's the old lady's name?

PIG

Epstein, filled with aspirin, Delancy Street. Come on Kong, there's no traffic now, we'll be back in an hour, please man.

KARA

If you're bullshitting me, you're dead, you got that? I am not playing games, I mean you're dead!

PIG

Yeah, yeah, got it.

KARA

What about us, you're gonna get yourself arrested, and what about us? Send one of your boys, get Louie to do it. You leave here, you're not coming back.

PIG

Please Kara…

KONG

You shut up.

DOT

You playing or not playing?

KARA

I'm in, just wait a second. (*to PIG*) Listen you son-of-a-bitch, this man served time for you once, he's not doing it again. He's got a life now, why don't you just leave us alone?

PIG

It's a kid, it's not me, I screwed up, okay, okay, I'm sorry, I'm sorry…I didn't mean…

KONG

Shut it, both of you. Finish your game. Kara. I'll be back in an hour.

DOT

I'm dealing.

KONG

Go.

KARA

Don't come back here, you leave, don't come back.

KONG

This is my house, that I built with my blood, you don't tell me what to do.

KARA

Fine, lose it all for this, Pig. You are so fucking dumb.

PIG

Please, I'm sorry...

KONG

Can you drive, hey, can you drive?

PIG

Yeah, I can drive.

KONG

I'm gonna work my biceps in the car. (*Picking up dumbbells*) You're not fucking with me?

PIG

No man, I swear.

KONG

Look at me. You're not fucking with me?

PIG

No Kong.

KONG

Look at me and say it.

PIG

I am not fucking with you.

KARA

You're so stupid, I'll see you in jail. Thanks a lot Pig, for ruining our lives again.

PIG

Thank you, thank you.

KONG

Shut up.

(*Kong puts on his wrestling cape. Takes his two dumbbells and they exit*)

KARA

(*Sitting at game*) I'm in.

BABE

So that's your brother-in-law.

KARA

Yeah, the Pig.

BABE

He's kind of cute.

DOT

In a disgusting, hopeless sort of way.

KARA

Yeah, why don't you take him in?

DOT
Aren't you being a little rough on him?

KARA
Listen ladies I'm sorry…but DAMMIT! FUCKING DAMMIT! (*PAUSE*) Let's play, okay let's play.

BABE
What's up, honey?

KARA
It's okay, deal.

DOT
Yeah Kara what's up?

KARA
This kid…

DOT
The Pig…

KARA
Yeah the fucking Pig, and that's what he is, he screws us over every time. I don't want to talk about this shit. I don't want to ruin our card night.

BABE
It's okay honey, you want another beer?

KARA
Sure. This kid comes in and screws up our life every time. Kong served six months for him on Rikers Island, before Jenny was born.

DOT
Jesus.

KARA
He thought Paulie was going to night school. He picked him up and there was dope in the car. They got pulled over, a tail light out or

                    KARA, continued
some shit. The cops found the dope and fucking Kong said it was his, so fucking Pig Man could get a G.E.D. It was all bullshit, he never went to one class. So Kong missed his first daughter's birth. I was there giving birth alone and Kong was in Rikers Island, a fucking hell hole because of that little prick. I'm here counting food stamps, taking our daughter to jail to see daddy. Because of Pig. He's no good. No fucking good and tough guy Kong has this place in his heart for him. Dot, will you fucking deal.

                    DOT
It's okay, babe we don't have to play.

                    BABE
Deal. Dottie.

                    KARA
I know they're going to get busted tonight. I'm sorry ladies. All this brother love shit. Deal let's play cards.

                    FADE

                    (*Scene in Car*)

                    PIG
Thanks.

                    KONG
Yeah.

                    PIG
You want to hear the radio?

                    KONG
No.

                    PIG
I hate that rap crap, all angry and everything…Am I going the right way?

KONG

Yeah, you're doin' fine. Get on the Expressway, next right.

PIG

Oh man...

KONG

I don't want to hear about it.

PIG

Yeah okay. (*Long pause*) Over the Queensborough bridge, right?

KONG

Yeah, right. (*Pumping weights. Pause*)

PIG

I got a lot of respect for you, you know that, right?

KONG

Just drive.

PIG

Russ... I mean that rap shit, it's all, blah, blah, blah, and blah, blah, blah. (*Improvises black rap stuff like;*) "Motherfucker sat on my bitches bed, took out his dick and gave her head..."

KONG

Shut it, Pig

PIG

Russ...
(*No answer, pause*)
I really fucked up bad, I don't know what to do. You got kids, right?

KONG

Right.

PIG

What do you do with them, your kids, do you go to little league and stuff? (*Pause*) Russ?

KONG

Just drive.

PIG

Queens Boulevard to the bridge?

KONG

Yeah.

PIG

You are doing so good. Mom and dad would be so proud, TV and all, I seen you on TV. Kong, the king. I'm so proud of you.

KONG

We're gonna get the kid, then I drop you off, and I take the kid home and that's it, that's the end of it, Kara'll take care of her and you're on your own. You got that?

PIG

Yeah.

KONG

Yeah what?

PIG

I got it. (*Pause*) Listen man, you got no baby seat, so would it be okay if I held her back to the Island, to your house, then I'm gone. I swear I disappear. I swear. You drive back and I'll hold her, would that be okay? (*Pause*) Russ…

KONG

You are gonna pay for this shit, so bad, really bad, you don't do this shit to people.

PIG
I know, I know. I'm sorry, it's just a little girl. I'm sorry man.

NANCY
(*Voice (child) Lights up on Kong's face and youg girl.*)
I never knew my father, they told me right away I was their niece, my uncle was so cool, Uncle Kong, the king of the wrestlers, he would let me watch him shave his chest, and pump iron, Aunt Kara and I would watch him on TV getting slammed and best of all slamming people, tossing them out of the ring, out of the world, smashing chairs over their heads. We would sit in front of the TV, my cousins and I and Aunt Kara, and watch Kong kick ass. We'd prepare a huge dinner that he would eat in the middle of the night. Then we'd go to bed, I never heard him come in. He'd come home and eat and eat and eat. Steaks and mashed potatoes and a giant bowl of salad. In the morning we'd see the empty plates, just like on Christmas morning we'd see the empty glass of milk and cookie crumbs the way we would leave for Santa. Anyway, we'd be and be off to school before Kong woke up, Aunt Kara would say, don't wake the Kong, he pays the bills and loves us.
(FADE)

PIG
You know man, maybe I shouldn't go up there, I mean the cops could be there, I could wait around the corner, in the car. And you could run up and get her.

KONG
You go up and get her. If you're not back in five minutes I'm gone.

PIG
I miss you man, I really miss you.

KONG
I'm sure you do.

PIG
You remember when…

KONG

I don't want to hear it.

PIG

I was just gonna say…

KONG

Don't start on me.

PIG

WHAT AM I GONNA DO! (*Pause*) Kong. I know you don't want to hear it, I screwed up, I mean lots of times, but this is the worst, this is the end of the line. I don't want to die or go back to jail, I can't believe Rita's gone, I can't. We were just having fun, you know, then boom, it's morning and…

KONG

I don't want to hear it…

PIG

I know you don't. BUT IT COULD HAVE BEEN YOU! (*Pause*) I'm sorry for yelling. Thanks for helping me…and the kid.

KONG

Don't miss the turn off.

PIG

Could I stop and get some cigarettes?

KONG

No! I got a match tomorrow, you understand that?

PIG

I'm sorry, I was crying, it was hard to see. I'm okay.

KONG

Good.

PIG
I hope she didn't give the baby any aspirin, it's not so good for them. That's all she knows, aspirin, speed and beer. It's not so good for kids.

KONG
If there's a police car in front of her place you keep driving, you got that?

PIG
Oh Jesus.

KONG
You got that!

PIG
Yeah. (*Pause*) If I had a few hundred bucks, I could get the kid and go up to Grand Central Station and just get a train out of town, I mean any place far away, like out west, I got a friends out west. You could just drop me on Delancy and you could go back home, if I had a few hundred or maybe a grand, I could get a cab and stop and get some formula and a bottle, and we're gone, me and the baby. What do you think? Kong? Russ? What do ya think? Would that be okay?

KONG
No. I'll take the kid.

PIG
You got no baby seat. (*Pause*) You think I'm lyin', don't you.

KONG
Just drive or pull over and get out.

PIG
Yeah, yeah. I'm gonna turn it all around, I am. I can't take this crap anymore. It's hard, you know, with no money, no nothin'. This is a nice car Russ. Jesus, you got your shit together, I'm proud of you, I am. I could go back to school and get it all together. I could do that man, I could, I'm not stupid, I just need a little help, you know. I mean you got some help. From coach Brown, from your old lady, from

                              PIG, continued
mom and dad, nobody can do it alone. I mean I had Rita, we had plans to go out west, she was so damn beautiful, a fuckin' movie star, and look what happened.

                                   KONG
If you're gonna keep yappin', put on the radio.

                                   PIG
Why are you being such a prick?

                                   KONG
Pig, don't make me mad and keep the car between the lines.

                                   PIG
God, you can't even talk to me.

                                   KONG
When I get mad I hurt people. You think when those bastards kick me around I don't want to break them in half, and I can do it. I say no, Kong stay in control, that's what they pay me for. I'll get my shot. You got no control, you lose it all. If this is some kind of game you're playin' with me your gonna be really sorry, sorry you were ever born. You got that?

                                   PIG
Yeah. I'll turn the radio on, okay.

                                   KONG
Okay.

                                   PIG
And Kong, I am sorry I was born. You sure we can't stop for cigarettes?

            (*Music up. Fade. Lights up on old lady (Mrs. Epstein) in a chair,
                          humming a Yiddish type song.*)

                              MRS. EPSTEIN
                           (*Humming half singing*)
And the baby should sleep and the life goes on and the creeps should

MRS. EPSTEIN, continued

die in their sleep, cause morning comes no matter what, and the birdies sing such…such…Paulie.

(*Pig appears in doorway*)

PIG

Mrs. Epstein.

MRS. EPSTEIN

Thank God, thank you God.

PIG

I'm here to get Nancy.

MRS. EPSTEIN

Who?

PIG

The baby, Mrs. Epstein, the baby.

MRS. EPSTEIN

Oh the Shainehala. (*Yiddish slang*)

PIG

Yeah, where is she? I don't see her.

MRS. EPSTEIN

She was sleeping, I sang her to sleep.

PIG

Where, where did you put her to sleep? Where's the baby?

MRS. EPSTEIN

She was sleeping on the pillow, so nice to have a little baby here.

PIG

What did you do with her?

MRS. EPSTEIN

Not me, the police. I said don't wake her. I said she was my Shainehala, my baby, and…

PIG

…and what?

MRS. EPSTEIN

You want a beer, Paulie?

PIG

And what happened, where is she?

MRS. EPSTEIN

And they took her. Sound asleep, like an angel. I told them not to and they took her. Three policeman, two in uniform and one in a suit, a nice blue suit with a tie, so handsome. .

PIG

Jesus!

MRS. EPSTEIN

I'm sorry, Paulie. What could I do?

PIG

What did they say? Did they mention my name?

MRS. EPSTEIN

No, no, nothing about you. The one in the suit said they had to take the child. He said they'd take good care of her. Oh, here, he left his card.

PIG

I got to go, my brother's waiting downstairs.

MRS. EPSTEIN

So he can't come up and have a beer with us?

PIG
You're sure she's not here.

MRS. EPSTEIN
No, no, they took her. Oh. They asked if I knew the mother or the father, I said no I don't know, and I don't know.

PIG
I got to go.

MRS. EPSTEIN
You be a good boy, Paulie, and bring her by any time, I'm a good Nana.

PIG
Yeah, thanks. (*Exiting*)

MRS. EPSTEIN
Maybe you could spare a few dollars…

(*FADE. Back in Car*)

KONG
What's goin' on?

PIG
Oh man, oh man, the cops took her.

KONG
The what? You're playin games with me, aren't you, aren't you!

PIG
No, no. The cops came and took my kid. Fuck. Here's the guy's card…

KONG
Gimme that. Lieutenant Frick. You had this the whole time, you planned this whole thing.

PIG
No, I didn't plan anything, no Kong, no, no, no…

MRS. EPSTEIN
(*Voice yelling out the window*) Paulie, Paulie, they forgot her hat, her little hat, here it comes. (*a baby hat falls onto the stage*)

PIG
Look, look man, you see, you see. Let's get her.

KONG
How the hell are we gonna do that?

PIG
We can do it, we can…

KONG
Yeah, walk into the precinct like it's a daycare center and say I'm here to pick up my daughter. I'm goin' home to sleep.

PIG
Listen to me, let me think for a second, don't go okay? We say we left the kid with this woman, Rita, the baby sitter. And we found a note, no, no, a piece a paper with Epstein's address on it and she gave us your card and we're here to get our kid.

KONG
And who are you, and how are you going to prove it's your kid…

PIG
I DON'T KNOW! OKAY! OKAY! I DON'T GODDAM KNOW! I don't know…(*crying*).

KONG
You know what I think, I think this is just a normal day for you. Your whole life is one big emergency.

PIG
It gets worse and worse and worse...

KONG
Have you had enough, have you?

PIG
Let's get my kid, let's get my baby, please...

KONG
HAVE YOU HAD ENOUGH! (*Getting PIG in a hammer lock*) HAVE YOU!

PIG
You're hurting me man, you're hurting me...Jesus...

KONG
That's right Pig, I'm fucking hurting you...Now you listen to me. I'm takin' you back to Rockaway, against my better judgment. I should let you die in the street, or get the electric chair for killing your old lady...

PIG
I didn't...

KONG
Shut up, or I'll kill you right here and get it over with.

PIG
My ki...

KONG
They'll take care of her better than you can, she probably needs a doctor and...

PIG
We got to get her, she's all I...

KONG
Shut up!

                          PIG

Russ, I'm strung out, I need a few…a few…a few rocks, two blocks away, two blocks man…please.,.please…twenty bucks man…

                          KONG

Where the fuck…do you think I'm carrying any money?

                          PIG

I don't know, I don't Goddam know, a credit card in the glove compartment, there's an ATM on First Avenue, I'd be quick, I would…

                          KONG

I'm goin', you come with me, or not, I don't know you, EVER…it's your choice.

                        BLACK OUT

                       END OF ACT 1

                          ACT II

(The KONG HOME, KARA watching match on TV. We hear the match. PIG enters in one of Kong's robes)

                          PIG

Hey Kara. *(Referring to robe)* He said it was okay. *(Pause)* Kara?

                          KARA

What?

                          PIG

Would it be okay if I finished up those chips?

                          KARA

No, it wouldn't.

                          PIG

Yeah, okay. How's he doing? *(Eating chips)*

KARA

Getting knocked around. Losing. He's suppose to lose. You're not suppose to be in here.

PIG

I had to use the bathroom, is that okay?

KARA

No, I don't want you in here.

PIG

I know you don't. I can't sleep in the car, it's damp and it smells from Ben-Gay.

KARA

Well, that's too bad.

PIG

Can I just sit in the chair for a minute, my back hurts. (*Eats some more chips*)

KARA

I told you…

PIG

I'm hungry, really hungry. I lost my daughter, the cops have her, did he tell you?

KARA

Yes, he told me.

PIG

And Rita…

KARA

He told me all about it. I don't want you here. You shouldn't be in our house.

PIG
He's taking lots of steroids, isn't he?

KARA
He does what he has to do…

PIG
Kara, I…you look really good, healthy. In that nightgown, you look great, really good, can I have some pretzels, they're really pretty stale.

KARA
Eat up and get out, take them with you.

PIG
Kara. (*Pause*) Do you have any orange juice, or a vitamin C tablet, I'm deficient in Vitamin C, can I have one of these Flintstones?

KARA
Listen Pig, they're for the kids.

PIG
Yeah. I'll need a few. (Pause, eats vitamins) You ever wake up with a dead person, it's weird, I mean…

KARA
Look at that! (*TV*) Jesus! He's hurt, his back, oh shit…

PIG
Hey Kara, it's a show, all make believe. These things taste pretty good, I just ate a Wilma. I heard the steroids screw up your sex life, is that true? That's what I heard.

KARA
He can't get up!

PIG
How can they lock up a three month old, I don't get it…

KARA

He's hurt, I can tell…

PIG

He's just good, he's kiddin' around, he use to pull that all the time. When we were kids I'd be beatin' the crap out him, he'd start cryin', I'd let him up then he'd nail me, get me every time, real tears and stuff, then bam, he'd nail me…and…

KARA

I'm tellin' you he's hurt, Rhino's gonna slam him again…Jesus…

PIG

Hey Kara, why don't you like me?

KARA

Jesus, it's over. Oh he's hurt, look at that, now that asshole is gonna dive off the ropes…JESUS RHINO, GIVE IT UP! A fucking commercial.

PIG

Why don't you like me?

KARA

What!

PIG

Why don't you like me?

KARA

I don't know, I don't give a damn about you.

PIG

Well yeah, that's what I mean.

KARA

Why don't you just leave?

PIG

What about me makes you not give a damn? What personality trait that I have makes you not give a damn?

KARA

Listen Pig…

PIG

Don't call me that!

KARA

You're a leech, you use people, you're a nobody, a train wreck, a disaster, a nothing.

PIG

Yeah, well if you knew me better, you might change your opinion.

KARA

Get away from me, he comes home he's gonna kill you.

PIG

Really. What about it, what about the steroids, do they screw up your sex life?

KARA

He's gonna kill you. His back, look at that, they're carryin' him off, he's really hurt, it was too short, the damn match was too short, he's really hurt, Goddamn it! What a lousy way to earn a living, poor bastard. Shit! Maybe I can get them on the phone…

PIG

(*Moving close to her*) Hey Kara, he's okay, it's gonna be okay, come here, honey, calm down.

KARA

Get away from me. I swear he's gonna kill you.PIG
Yeah, well, I have one advantage, I want to die.

(BLACK OUT)

(LIGHTS UP)

(Enter KONG, hurting, wearing neck brace. PIG passed out on the couch.)

KARA
You okay, honey?

KONG
I'm hurtin', I'm okay, I got half-paid, it got cut short, the match, I hurt my back, my neck, gimme some codeine.

KARA
Yeah, yeah. The kids are at Dot's. You gonna be okay?

KONG
I don't know. What's he doin' in here?

KARA
He was hungry, what could I do? He ate the crap from the card game. You okay?

KONG
Yeah, my neck hurts.

KARA
I love you babe, I'll get you an ice pack…

KONG
Make me my steak, and get me a beer. *(Exit KARA)* HEY PIG!

PIG
Yeah. *(Waking up)*

KONG
I'm gonna give you a thousand dollars to get out of my life. That's it pal. Here you go. (*Takes out big roll of bills*). Call a cab and go. Here's the newspaper, they found Rita. It says here she was a semi-famous folk singer in the Village coffee houses.

PIG
Yeah, she was. She was good. Semi-famous, semi-love songs.

KONG
So what did she want with you?

PIG
I'm a good fuck.

KONG
Jesus, my neck…Excuse me, what did you say?

PIG
I think you heard me, we all have our skills.

KONG
Did you see my match?

PIG
Yeah, part of it. You're good, Kara was scared, you're good. I helped her out, from her fear…you know. Can I take the Buick, and leave, I mean you have the other car.

KONG
You son of a bitch. (*Tries to grab PIG*). Ouch! You never stop, do you. You never stop your fuckin' hustle, do you?

PIG
The upholstery stinks from Ben-Gay, that's a strong smell in a Buick.

KONG
Three weeks, three goddam weeks I got to lay off. That's a lot of money pal. That's a big loss.

PIG
I could go in for you.

KONG
Yeah, I don't think so.

PIG
Yeah, I used to beat the shit out of you. You remember?

KONG
Not really.

PIG
Listen Russ, I wear the wig and the make up, and I do it. You feed me some good food and pump me with steroids and speed for a week. I'll kick anybody's ass.

KONG
You're nuts, you wouldn't last two minutes.

PIG
I would man, I really would, I'd do good.

KONG
One body slam, you'd be in the hospital.

PIG
So what, I like the hospital, nurses, white stockings, IV in your arm and reach under their skirts when they put the needle in, I like that. Morphine, it's great. Listen Russ, I'll do anything to get some money, I don't give a shit. I want my kid, and I'll find out where she is, and I'll take care of her. I don't even know where Rita's funeral is. I can't even go to my wife's funeral, that's some fucked up shit. I'll go on the damn TV and kick ass. But you got to feed me man and explain what's going on in the ring. I'll give you most of the money.

KONG
You can't go in as me.

PIG

Not as you, "The Son of Kong", revenge. It's drama, man. But you got to talk to me, tell me the moves, the game. You know, teach me. (*Pause*) Can I have a drink, would that be okay?

KONG

In the cabinet, but make it fast.

PIG

I swear to God I'll do it. And I have a great advantage…

KONG

WHERE'S MY STEAK! KARA! What's that Pig, what do you have?

PIG

I don't give a shit. So nobody can hurt me. Not Rhino or God or anybody. Please man, let me do it. Rita would be so proud, Nancy, my baby, would be so proud, then I'd earn the money to take her out West, that's a good start. I wear your wig, it would put me into your head, your brain. Let me try it on, please man. (*PIG grabs KONG'S blond wig*) Yeah, yeah, (*Dancing around with wig on*) Son of Kong, you breathe you die. I AM THE SON OF KONG AND I BREATHE THE FIRE OF REVENGE! I swear, nobody can hurt me more than I've been hurt. How do you keep this thing on?

KONG

I'd love to see you get your ass kicked and your back broken…

PIG

So let me do it, come on man. I look good don't I? Kong, come on, babe.

KONG

Why you wearing my robe?

KARA

(*Entering with beer*) He said, you said he could wear it.

PIG

I put my clothes in the washing machine, they were stinkin'…Could I get a beer too? So what do you say, Kong?

KARA

What's he want now?

KONG

He wants to go in and wrestle for me.

KARA

I'd like to see that.

PIG

You see Russ, what could happen, I get killed, great, that would be great, I'd be with Rita, I'd be off your back, you'd get plenty of publicity, "Brother of Kong dies for him." Then all your matches are all revenge, you'd be the good guy. Everyone would be rooting for you. You'd be King, King Kong.

KARA

Yeah, what if you just got crippled, we'd have to take care of you for the rest of your life. What a pain in the ass that would be.

PIG

No, no, I'd call that guy, you know the death doctor, Kevorkian, and have him put me out, like we had to do with Laddie…

KARA

Who?

KONG

Our dog, when we were kids, he got hit by a car, it was two hundred bucks to have him fixed up, so they put him to sleep.

PIG

Bastards! I told the damn vet I'd work it off, clean cages, walk the dogs, anything. He said no, I was too young, mom and dad said no,

PIG, continued

he's an old dog, so they put him to sleep. Cheap bastards, it was our dog, right Kong?

(*PIG reaches for one of Kara's cigarettes and lights it.*)

Is it okay if I take a goddamn smoke?

KARA

No!

KONG

Let him have it.

PIG

And a beer?

KONG

Get him a beer.

KARA

You know what he tried to do, He tried to…

KONG

I don't give a damn. Get it.

KARA

You're so dumb.

KONG

Get it.

KARA

I'd like to see him get his ass kicked, his head broken in.

PIG

Yeah, what if I win?

KONG

Don't worry, you wouldn't win. It's all planned out, they never let a new guy win. And you couldn't win if they let you.

PIG

You know, you don't know a thing about the human spirit. I am "Son of Kong."

KARA

The Pig Man.

PIG

A cross between a Pig and the King of Apes. Who's your next match?

KONG

Get off it, you're not doin' it.

PIG

Who?

KONG

The Bear, a giant hairy bastard who weighs four hundred pounds. He'd eat you alive.

PIG

Fine, let him. I want to be eaten. You adopt my daughter, and I die in the claws of the Bear. If I win who's next?

KONG

Take the grand and go. I got a headache.

KARA

Will you leave him alone?

PIG

Who's next? A rematch with Rhino, that's it isn't it! I'll kick his ass for hurting you, I swear to God, man.

KONG

It wasn't his fault, I fell wrong, because I wasn't thinking, he whispered the move in my ear and I wasn't ready. We were supposed to do forty minutes and we did twenty, they're all pissed at me.

KARA

Because you spent half the night out with him, because you didn't get your sleep, he kept you up all night, you couldn't concentrate. You're a sucker, Kong.

KONG

Give me a fuckin' break Kara. Is my steak ready. Is it!

KARA

In a minute. Stupid ass, you let this creep screw up our lives, like he screws everything up. Jesus…

(*Exit Kara. PAUSE.*)

PIG

Russ?

KONG

Yeah.

PIG

You really think they're takin' care of her, my kid?

KONG

I think so, how do I know?

PIG

Please. Let me do this. Let me know what it feels like, to be you. You were cryin' like a bastard when they put Laddie down, and they wouldn't let me do shit, nothin'. I begged them, like I'm beggin' you. Let me clean up the animal shit, and always no, no, no, no. So I fall and fall again and I don't give a shit, and I lose because I'm numb, and I wake up to a frozen woman and a crying baby. Rita would say; "Find an enemy, an enemy that's not you." Russ, she was so damn good, and I don't feel anything except what I think I'm suppose to feel. I want to feel the physical feeling of hurt, of pain, of death, man. I worked in car wash, I lasted less than an hour, the asshole said you're over-qualified. I was a messenger, I lasted less then a day, I stole ten dollars and that was it. I tried lots of shit, but I couldn't do it.

KONG
And you want to fight for me.

(PIG and KONG take a long look at each other)
KONG
KARA, GIVE PIG MY SHOT!

(KARA enters with steak)

KARA
What are you talkin' about?

KONG
Give the Pig Man here my shot. This looks good (*Steak*) Kara, black. Give him the shot.

KARA
You sure, babe?

KONG
I'm sure.

KARA
You're sure.

KONG
Yes, do it!

PIG
I'm gonna kick ass, you'll see. Do I get a wax job? And the tanning bed, the whole deal?

KONG
The whole deal. You're gonna die or get your or neck or back broken, and I'm gonna watch it on TV, right in our bedroom. And I'm gonna laugh my ass off.

PIG
We got a week, right?

KONG
Four days.

PIG
You'll teach me, right, talk me through it, It's all phony, right?

KONG
Yeah, like a little play, all phony.

PIG
You'll tell me how to fall, there's a trick to it, right?

KONG
Yeah, it's all a trick, a show.

PIG
I can do it, I know I can do it. I mean, I'm not in such good shape, but if you can do it, I can do it. Fuck, I'll kick ass.

KONG
Kara, give him the shot.

PIG
Yeah Kara, do it. Russ? Kara? You'll get my kid for me, right?

KARA
Turn around and show me your ass, it's steroids and vitamins. You're sure, babe?

KONG
Do it.

(Kara *injects Pig in the ass*)

PIG
That's it?

KONG
Before the match we'll give you some speed.

PIG

And a costume, I mean my body looks like shit, I need a costume so I look scary, so I feel scary.

KARA

We'll fix you up, won't we, Kong? Here's your ice pack, babe.

PIG

SON OF KONG, the King of the bad asses. What's my match? Who?

KONG

I told you, The Bear.

PIG

The Bear eats it, the bear dies, everything I touch dies! You'll get my baby, right? Right!

KONG

Come here, Pig, come here. (*Whispering*) We'll get the kid.

(*KONG smashes him one to the head*)

PIG

Jesus, man.

KONG

Pay attention, lesson one. Babe, lets go to bed. Goodnight Pig.

(*KARA helps KONG off couch, they start to exit.*)

PIG

I don't think I can sleep, I'm all worried about Nancy, do you have anything to help me sleep, you must have something in the house, something, I'm all worried. HEY! (*Pause*) I can't sleep without Rita. I'm scared, okay, okay? Can I have one of Kong's painkillers? Russ?

KONG

No.

PIG
I'm just asking, okay? I thought you being hurt and all.

KARA
Sleep tight, Pig Man.

KONG
In the car.

(They Exit)

PIG
(Taking blankets off couch.)
Yeah, yeah, Yeah. Sleep in the car? Fuck that, I'll sleep with my brother, I'll do his wife, no, he's a good guy, the Kong, I can't be alone, I can't be alone. Cut the shit, man. If only I had some strong sleeping pills, there must be something here to help me sleep. I'll get the kid back, it all works out. Black curly hair with blue eyes, she's a beauty, Rita. That shot did shit, nothing. HEY KONG!

KONG
(Off stage)

Shut up!

PIG
I can't sleep.

KONG
(Back on stage half dressed, hands PIG three pills.)
Go to sleep! They're Perks, for my pain, not yours.

PIG
Can I sleep with you? I'm scared man, I don't feel so good. Can I sleep with you and Kara?

KONG
No, now fuck off and go to sleep.

HALF LIGHTS

(PIG in Chair. Voice of KARA and KONG)

KARA
You really gonna let him do it?

KONG
Yeah. Screw it.

KARA
He's gonna make a fool of himself.

KONG
Good.

KARA
I know you care about him.

KONG
Not really. He's my brother. Stupid ass that he is. Oh man, my neck.

KARA
You gonna be okay?

KONG
Yeah, they X-rayed it, nothing's broken. I hate to lose the money, I mean for us.

KARA
We'll be okay.

KONG
Yeah, we'll buy a car wash, then a whole bunch of them all over the Island. The Kong Wash, hot wax, the whole deal, automated. We'll just collect the money. We're gonna do okay. I'm gonna get his kid. That okay with you?

KARA
Yeah, as long as you don't get in trouble. It's a baby, right?

KONG
Yeah, Nancy, a little girl. She didn't do anything to anybody. It's not her fault.

KARA
Yeah babe, it's okay.

(*PAUSE*)

PIG
KONG!

KONG
Jesus, WHAT!

PIG
CAN I PLEASE SLEEP ON THE COUCH, PLEASE! THE BUICK STINKS FROM BEN-GAY AND GASOLINE!

KONG
FINE, JUST SHUT IT!

PIG
(*Pause*) RUSS?

KONG
WHAT!

PIG
THANKS! (*Pause*) I LIKE THE WIG! (*Pause*) KARA!

KARA
WHAT!

PIG
GOODNIGHT!

                    KONG
SHUT IT MAN!

          Sound of KARA and KONG laughing)

                    PIG
YOU GUYS LAUGHING?

                    KONG
CRYING!

                    KARA
WE'RE CRYING. FOR YOU!

                    KONG
NOW GO TO SLEEP!

                    PIG
OKAY! I'M TRYING!

                    KONG
What did he try to do to with you?

                    KARA
Nothing, really, nothing.

                    PIG
I LOVE YOU GUYS!

                    KONG
SHUT IT!

          (Pig getting into costume, dancing around.)

                    PIG
First I dance around, prance around like I own the damn ring. Why do they call it a ring? It's a square, square, they're all so square. So I look at the audience, like, SCREW YOU JERKS! HEY BEAR! UGLY HAIRY BASTARD, YOU DIE TONIGHT.

KONG
SHUT IT!

PIG
And I give him the finger, and prance around and throw something at the hairy bastard, some kind of rosin and shit and like he's getting pissed off and I prance around like I own the place and he comes at me and I kick him in the balls like right off, to show him I'm not kidding around. The Pig Man has no rules. Oh yeah…

KONG
WHO YOU TALKING TO? GO TO SLEEP.

PIG
(*Pause*) I am so sick of losing, all the time, everything, because I'm the smart one, and I get fucked, every time, everywhere, all the time, yeah, YEAH!

KONG
SHUT UP! GO SLEEP IN THE CAR!

KARA
YOU'RE BUGGING US!

PIG
(*Softer*) Because I'm trying to do good, but get screwed over and over again. It's Pig against Paulie all the fucking time. No format, man. Me against me, that's not a fair match, it's always a stalemate. I had no format man…(*Looking around*) But now I have the Bear and Rhino and some formidable assholes to kick. Fuck their rules, they kill me, they kill me. Me and Rita screwing in the hereafter for eternity, that's hot man, really hot news. REALLY HOT!

KONG
THAT'S IT PAULIE! (*entering*) Into the garage, go. (*grabbing PIG by the neck*).

PIG
Oh man. (*gagging, KONG lets him go*) You know, I could break you in half, I always could. Couldn't I?

KONG

No, no more. You want to fuck with me? Do you? DO YOU!

PIG

No.

KONG

Go to sleep.

PIG

I'm sorry Kong, Russ, I mean it. I don't mean any harm to you and…

KONG

Paulie, listen to me. I'm gonna say this once. I can't fuck up my life for you. I can't screw my family over, like mom and dad did to us. I can't do it. I got Kara, I got good kids…

PIG

I got a kid too. Jesus, Russ.

KONG

I could have been like you. In fact deep down I am like you but I care about something that's not me. Listen to me, something outside myself. You think about that little girl, she needs you. You forget about the dope, you put Paulie aside. You put that little girl first. You know how I use to like to get high?

PIG

Yeah. You're the one who first turned me on. You remember the night when…

KONG

I'm sorry Paulie I'm sorry I did that.

PIG

Yeah, but it made us tight, me and you. That was the best night of my life. The first time I didn't feel alone.

KONG
You're not alone, Paulie. You think I would put up with your shit if I didn't care about you. I was fucking glad when you were born, I figured I had a pal, a brother. Anyone try to fuck with you, I'd kick their ass, including big shot prick daddy.

PIG
Why was he so fucking mean?

KONG
It doesn't matter, he had his problems, something screwed him over too. It's over with. He's dead. They're both dead. Get over it.

PIG
Can you say it? Please. Like when we were kids.

KONG
I'm me, you're you, we're blood. I love you, Paulie, no matter what. (*Pause*) Now fuckin' go to sleep.

PIG
Kong I'm gonna try. I'm gonna try real hard. For Nancy and for Rita and for you, too.

KONG
Goodnight, Paulie.

PIG
Yeah. Kong, (*Pause*) thank you.

KONG
Come on lay down, I'll cover you up.

KARA
KONG!

KONG
YEAH!

KARA

COME TO BED!

KONG

GIVE ME A FUCKIN' BREAK! (*Tucking PIG in*) You okay?

PIG

Funny thing is I miss our dog more than I miss mom and dad. You too?

KONG

I don't think about it.

PIG

That's good Russ, to not think.

KONG

Good night.

PIG

Yeah.

(*BLACK OUT*)

(*LIGHTS UP*)

KONG
(*Looking out window*)
The car is gonna be here any minute. You remember what I told you?

PIG

Yeah, yeah. I'm good. All the money is yours.

KONG

You break your fall with your arms, you got that?

PIG

Yeah, yeah. I'm good.

                    KONG

The Bear'll tell you what's coming, just do what he says. Keep an eye on the guys in your corner and the Ref.

                    PIG

You have the number, where they're holding Nancy.

                    KARA

We have it.

                    PIG

Just go and see if she's okay, you'll do that? Do I look good?

                    KONG

You're okay. Paulie, the car's here.

                    PIG

I'm doin' good. One more hit. (*Takes a hit of coke*) The SON OF KONG KICKS ASS!

                    KONG

Don't be a wise guy. Do what they tell you. You understand?

                    PIG

The SON OF KONG!

                    KONG

Paulie, don't be a smart ass or you'll get hurt bad, pay attention to Bear, he'll tell you what to do.

                    PIG

THE SON OF KONG KICKS ASS!

                (*PIG Exits*)

                    KARA

Bear's gonna waste him.

KONG

Bear's a pro, ex-fighter, he'll take care of him, toss him around like a baby.

KARA

He's gonna get hurt. He's too dumb to follow advice, I see it in his face. He thinks it's a real fight.

KONG

He'll be fine.

KARA

Russ?

KONG

Yeah?

KARA

Let me go get the baby. I can do it. I'll say I'm the kids aunt, I'll take care of her. He's gonna come back all broken up. We'll have his kid here when he gets back.

KONG

It's not that simple.

KARA

I can do it. I'm good at that stuff, I am, talking to authorities. I'm good at it. We'll take care of the kid, what's one more kid?

KONG

What did he do to you?

KARA

He didn't do anything.

KONG

But you want to take his baby.

KARA

It's a baby. It's not my baby. It's just a baby. Your brother's baby.

KONG
You think you can do it?

KARA
Yeah, I do. I'm a good talker. Please Russ, it's family.

KONG
Then do it.

KARA
I'll take the Buick, okay?

KONG
Yeah.

KARA
You okay?

KONG
Yeah.

KARA
You want an ice pack?

KONG
I'm okay.

(*BLACK OUT*)

ANNOUNCER
They say that professional wrestling is all phony. Well, this man, and he is a man, The Son of Kong, was pronounced dead, two minutes ago, by Doctor Steinbeck, the ring doctor. Son of Kong died of head contusions and a broken neck, blood cut off to the brain, it is the first death in professional wrestling in over fifty years. It is said that he is not the son of Kong but his younger brother, who wanted to go in for his older brother. We hear Kong can't wait to pay back for his brothers' death and we're all behind him. What a hero, the son, I should say the brother of Kong. We look forward to Kong's return. You have witnessed professional wrestling's first death.

(LIGHTS DOWN, UP ON NANCY)

NANCY
He is so much fun, Kong is. In the summer we run through the wash, the car wash, all the puffy, spinning stuff, me and my cousins. He has twenty car washes now, The Kong Wash, best wash on the island. On Saturday mornings we go and empty the money out of the boxes. They have been really honest with me, my dad sounds like a pretty great guy, they said he was really strong and loved me a lot. Paulie, I know they called him Pig. I have a tape of my mom singing, it's not the music I like, not much of a beat, but she has a nice voice, and there are all these nice words about the snow and birds and how people should try to care about each other, I guess she was pretty good, not much of a beat. Uncle Russ had to have surgery on his back and his knees, he's fifty now. I play the violin, and we have a dog named Laddie, we got him from the pound. When I hit certain notes on the violin he tries to sing with the notes I play. I like that. It's mostly around the high "D" and the high "E". I guess the high notes do something to a dog. In some ways I feel all alone. But when I read books, the words on the page, I know we're all part of the same thing. I'm sorry daddy and mommy died before I got to know them, but hey, I'm having fun, so that's good, right?

(Lights start Slow Fade)

KONG
(Voice)
NANCY!

NANCY
Yeah, Uncle Russ.

KONG
It's time to go. You ready, honey? You're not nervous are you, your first recital and all?

NANCY
I'm okay, I'm all set, I know the piece.

KONG
KARA!

KARA
THE KIDS ARE IN THE CAR!

KONG
Nancy, you're gonna do great.

NANCY
Thanks for new violin and the new dress, it makes me feel really good.

KONG
Thank the Kong Wash.

NANCY
Thank you Kong Wash.

KONG
And thank your mom and dad, for the talent, Paulie and Rita.

NANCY
Yeah, (*Pause*) thanks, mom and dad.

KONG
Paulie and Rita.

NANCY
Yeah. Uncle Russ, we better go.

KONG
Yeah.

FADE TO BLACK, MUSIC UP.

END OF PLAY

Curbdivers of Redemption

Curbdivers of Redemption 1997

First production, Contois Auditorium,
Burlington, VT
Directed by the author

Original Cast

Madge – Tracey Girdich
Thomas – Bob Bolyard
Esther – Elana Aubrey
Professor – Paul Schnabel
Alley – Craig Parish
Babe – Adriano Shaplin
Sam – Josh Bridgman
Johnson – Peter Seguin
Detective – Jordan Gullikson
Malcolm – Jordon Gullikson
Director – Jordan Gullikson

Cast of Characters

Madge – Sexy medicated housewife.
Thomas – Insurance salesman, Madge's husband.
Esther – Horny next door neighbor.
Professor – Stuart, charming down and out alcoholic, British movie star.
Alley – Wise street drunk.
Babe – Ex-boxer.
Sam – Ambitious street drunk.
Detective Shields – New York cop.
Malcolm – Art store salesman.
Director – Big time Hollywood Director.

Curbdivers of Redemption

ACT I
Scene 1
SETTING: A living room
AT RISE: MADGE and THOMAS

THOMAS
Madge, dinner?

MADGE
A roast.

THOMAS
The vegetable?

MADGE
Okra and potatoes broiled to perfection in the gravy, in the blood.

THOMAS
Madge, undo my tie. Madge, undo my tie. The fruit?

MADGE
Melon balls.

THOMAS
Melon balls, chilled?

MADGE
Of course chilled.

THOMAS
Not frozen.

MADGE
No. Freezing depletes the vitamins.

THOMAS
Kiss?

MADGE
A kiss, for Thomas, the hard-working insurance salesman. Wet?

THOMAS
Dry, on the lips. (*Kiss*) The children tucked in?

MADGE
Tucked in and kissed and loved and read to.

THOMAS
Candles?

MADGE
Red.

THOMAS
Wine.

MADGE
White, chilled.

THOMAS
Dessert?

MADGE
Heated apple turnovers with a scoop of vanilla, low fat ice cream.

THOMAS
Coffee.

MADGE
Cappuccino, decaffeinated.

THOMAS
Sex?

MADGE
Bath done, diaphragm in. Clean and fast, me on top, vibrator after.

THOMAS
Sheets.

MADGE
Silk and dry cleaned.

THOMAS
Mail.

MADGE
Read and filed.

THOMAS
Bills.

MADGE
Paid.

THOMAS
Dog.

MADGE
Walked, flea bath at vet.

THOMAS
Goldfish.

MADGE
Fed, filter cleaned.

THOMAS
Car.

MADGE
Volvo wagon, washed and vacuumed, hot waxed.

THOMAS
Air bags.

MADGE
Secure.

THOMAS
Love me?

MADGE
Love you, Thomas.

THOMAS
Love you, Madge.

MADGE
Name.

THOMAS
Madge. Name.

MADGE
Thomas.

THOMAS
Tomorrow's dinner. Madge?

MADGE
Turkey breasts, boneless, late flowering broccoli.

THOMAS
Grain.

MADGE
Grain, grain? Grain?

THOMAS
GRAIN.

MADGE
Grain? Tomorrow's grain?

THOMAS
Yes, what is it? What!

MADGE
Tomorrow, what is it?

THOMAS
WHAT! FOR GOD'S SAKES!

MADGE
Buckwheat kernels.

THOMAS
Last night was buckwheat. GRAIN!

MADGE
My God! Wheat berries.

THOMAS
That was Tuesday. GRAIN, THURSDAY! WHAT IS IT? WHAT!

MADGE
ORGANIC BROWN SHORT GRAIN RICE!

THOMAS
NO! THAT WAS MONDAY. THURSDAY!

MADGE
Thursday?

THOMAS
GRAIN, BITCH. THURSDAY'S GRAIN!

MADGE
I can't think of it. I'm sorry.

THOMAS
STUPID BITCH! Are you a stupid bitch? ARE YOU? A stupid bitch who can't plan ahead. ARE YOU?

MADGE
I do my best.

THOMAS
Love me? Your best?

MADGE
Yes, my best.

THOMAS
Do you love me? Say it, say it.

MADGE
I love you.

THOMAS
Say my name.

MADGE
Thomas, I love you…prick.

THOMAS
What did you say?

MADGE
I said, I love you, THOMAS…little, ugly, turtle prick.

THOMAS
Tomorrow's dinner.

MADGE
Warmed serrated grapefruit, to start with.

THOMAS

Sex, tomorrow.

MADGE

Backwards with the movie of the women. Tabouli, the grain is tabouli.

THOMAS

Well, thank you. Tabouli, tabouli is fine. House number.

MADGE

Seven, seven, seven.

THOMAS

No, Madge. Where's your mind? Where's your mind, dreaming? Drifting?

MADGE

One, one, one.

THOMAS

No, Madge.

MADGE

Nine, nine, nine.

THOMAS

Nine, nine, nine is right. Same as Volvo plate but with what?

MADGE

Two ones, nine, nine, nine, one, one.

THOMAS

Dinner, Madge, serve dinner. For Christ's sake serve dinner. SERVE ME MY GOD GIVEN DINNER. What the hell are you waiting for?

MADGE

I don't know.

(*Lights cross fade*)

Scene 2

SETTING: Alleyway
AT RISE: MEN softly pounding cartons like bass drums, from the inside.
(ALLEY and SAM, with great effort, crawl out of cartons.)

SAM
It's simple; we go out to the fuckin' suburbs and paint numbers.

ALLEY
Yeah...give me a hit...paint numbers...paint numbers.

SAM
Yeah, paint numbers on the curb, in front of the house. You ring the bell and say, twenty bucks for the number.

ALLEY
What number?

SAM
The house, the number for Christ's sakes, the number on the house, you don't even fuckin' ask, it's so simple. You say everyone on the block has them. That's the key; everyone on the block has them.

ALLEY
You're telling me they're all gonna give us twenty bucks?

SAM
Yeah we could clean up. You paint the number first...then say twenty bucks.

ALLEY
For Christ's sakes Sammy...numbers...numbers.

SAM
I've done it. I've made a lot of money.

ALLEY
Numbers.

SAM

Yeah, numbers okay? I've made plenty. You have no interest, fine; fuck you and your sister. Me and this guy used to do it all the time – two, three hundred bucks a day, so fuck you.

ALLEY

Yeah, big fuckin' dreams. You've got big fuckin' dreams Sammy and you know where they get you? Right fuckin' here! Hey Sammy, where you gonna get the paint?
(*PAUSE*)
You got any fuckin' paint? I don't see any paint. You got nothin', fuckin' zero. You don't even have a smoke, poor bastard.

SAM
(*BABE coming out of box*)

Hey Babe, this guy doesn't believe me about the house numbers. Babe, is that a scam or what? Nobody's done it for years. Was it the best?

BABE

The best, yeah. Where's my shoes? Where are my shoes…the numbers yeah…

SAM

This guy, this fuckin' guy won the Golden Gloves. What year, Babe, what year did you win the Gloves? He punished the guy. He kicked his ass. What year, Babe, what year?

BABE

Seventy-two. What of it? Jose Cortez, light middleweight. Kicked his fuckin' ass, broke his nose and two ribs.

SAM

He broke his nose and two ribs – three shots, bam, bam, bam…You get the paint in the paint store. You steal it. Babe, a left or a right, Alley, give me a hit.

ALLEY
There's nothing, nothing left. Dry city. I can't give you a hit. I'll give you a fuckin' hit right to the head. Hit him Babe. I'll break your head open.

BABE
Open up, bam, bam, bam, open up, no protection, fuckin' up, no shit. Open up, no more protection, you fuckin' attack, and hit, bam, right, the head, the brains, bam, gimme a drink.

ALLEY
Get away, get away man. There is gonzo, nothing left, all fuckin' gone.

SAM
Screw you guys. You've got no ambition. No fuckin' ambition to better yourselves, dry city.

(Bottles of wine come falling out of the other box, followed by a beat up man, PROFESSOR, with swollen eyes)

PROFESSOR
(British accent)
Cocktails are served, while we wait for God, who seems to be preoccupied with the trouble of the world…terrible responsibility to be God.

SAM
Where'd you get it? My God, professor.

PROFESSOR
Our God, a brick through a window into the store of spirits, the brick flew from my hand, the glass shattered and I entered and took, honestly prevailed, Shakespeare on my shoulder, a rider on the poetry of confusion, I filled this very canvas shopping bag, with the cheap stuff, sparing them bankruptcy, a few pints for the boys, I thought, the boys in the boxes. A few small cuts on the arm for humanity.

BABE

Any smokes?

PROFESSOR

Fags, of course. Ciggies in the box, cartons, Luckies, Camels, Pall Mall, Pell Mell and is well, yet another brick for the gentlemen of the night. Another brick through another window, it's only acting, my friends. We must be brave and not underestimate ourselves. Richard Burton said to me, "You take the part in your hand like a flower, like your prick and you don't fucking play games," and that is a direct quote. It was the three of us, Richard Burton, Richard Harris and myself in the pub and in the corner, Anthony Burgess not saying a word. Am I boring you my friends? The Japanese write and think about living in boxes, a wonderful book, *The Box Man*.

BABE

You stole my shoes, you fucker.

PROFESSOR

But for the cause, my dear Babe, smokes, wine and terror. Here are your shoes. All is well and good, peace and goodness prevail.

SAM

You just write the numbers. You fuckin' write the numbers. You guys don't get it, you get a, a, what do you call it? A, a, template so they look neat, you look at the house and a, a, template, you write down the fuckin' number on the curb. What could be easier?

BABE

Okay, who wants their ass kicked? Who wants it? I mean now.

SAM

The Gloves, he won the Golden Gloves. Babe, you are beautiful. Is this man beautiful? Is he beautiful?

BABE

And the fuckin' Olympics – don't forget that. I hated the headgear, then that big fuckin' nigger broke my jaw. He was out of his weight class. He was no light, middleweight. He was a fuckin' heavyweight.

BABE, continued

Cassius Clay broke my jaw. I saw that punch coming – couldn't get my arms up, just couldn't get it up. One fuckin' hit, easy, right arm up and block it, push it away, easy right arm block it, left hook and he dies. I could have broken his head open. A second too late – the fuckin' light hit my eyes and bam, it was over. The son of a bitch was out of his weight class. He was a heavyweight.

PROFESSOR

Babe, have some wine. To Mohammed.

BABE

I really got fucked.

SAM

Babe, some wine.

BABE

Yeah, yeah. I saw that punch, I saw it coming. The right arm, whack and the left hook. One fuckin' mistake, one fuckin' mistake. I saw that punch. It was nothing. Jive-ass hit, caught me right here. Right on the button. Lucky bastard…

SAM

Babe, we got wine.

PROFESSOR

Then Harris says to me, drunken bastard, he says, "You are the greatest actor the world will ever see," with that flair of his. We finished this movie, this stupid, bloody reel. I mean no content, nothing and these guys are getting millions and I get this stupid part. Oh, fuck you guys. I play this part of this pussy-whipped jerk. Harris is having an affair with my wife. Really bad writing, with Oliver Reed and the other sell-out cunts, the actors of England, with their winters in Barbados and Sir Gielgud says, "Stuart, change your name, Jews are very unpopular." Yes and Hitler thought so too! Those bloody fuckers, those…

ALLEY
Okay, okay, okay, you did a great job getting the wine and smokes.

SAM
Yeah, Professor, you're okay.

BABE
Yeah, fuckin' right on. You got balls. The professor has balls.

PROFESSOR
"Balls", said the queen, "If I had two I'd be the King." The Prince said, "I have two…"

SAM
You on board Prof, are you on board? I'm telling you, I'm a fuckin' sailor to the tenth. I can sail a fuckin' ship through anything, anytime – sails, motor, ketch, sloop. I don't give a shit. I can sail anything, anytime. I'll sail you fuckers to Africa and leave you there. I didn't cause any fuckin' oil spill, who do they blame? Me. Fuckin' me. Listen, the numbers, we can start tomorrow. Hit the F train – we'll get the paint in Queens. No sense in carrying the fuckin' paint on the train. By tomorrow night we're in hotel rooms ordering cocktails and steaks.

PROFESSOR
Sipping sangria off the coast of Spain. Gentlemen, oh, to paint beautiful pictures, beautiful pictures. Jasper Johns painted numbers and targets, numbers and targets and who, gentlemen, is keeping score?

ALLEY
Exactly. Who is keeping score?

SAM
With that fuckin' accent they can't say no. Let me hear you say it. Twenty bucks for the number. Come on, say it.

ALLEY
Come on baby, say it.

BABE

Yeah, come on, Professor.

PROFESSOR

We've painted your number, darling. That will be twenty dollars, cash.

SAM

Great!

ALLEY

Fuckin' right on!

PROFESSOR

Wait. Listen…so she says how about a cup of tea for you hard working gentlemen? We enter…she invites me up to the boudoir, the woman of the house – an estimate for a paint job.

BABE

Jesus.

PROFESSOR

A depraved, deprived, attractive housewife. Meanwhile you gentlemen steal the fucking place blind as I seduce the lady of the house.

SAM

No. No stealing. How do we carry the shit?

ALLEY

Shut up, Sammy.

PROFESSOR

The Volvo, we take the Volvo wagon. They all have them. Not much of an automobile, no power. The house will be a triple repeated odd number. Seven, seven, seven Something Place or nine, nine, nine Happiness Drive. I will purposely prolong her orgasm till I hear the engine start. I'll say, Madge or Midge or Mary, you are quite a woman, a wonderful lover. Just before she's able to apologize for the unsymmetrical balance of her breasts, as Liz many times apologized to me, off we go in the Volvo. Smooth as silk.

BABE

Now that's a fuckin' plan.

PROFESSOR

Thank you Babe.

ALLEY

The Professor's got class.

PROFESSOR

Samuel, the number painting is quite inventive and the word you were looking for is stencil, not template. A template is quite another animal.

BABE

I don't want to go back to the joint. No more jail. I hate fuckin' jail.

PROFESSOR

That was Olivier's problem, afraid to take chances. When I said, Lawrence, with all due respect, too much control, it's not interesting, he said…

BABE

I saw that fuckin' punch coming…

PROFESSOR

He said, "You'll never work again in bloody English Theater." Big fucking deal. I said, dear Sir Lawrence, why don't you go suck Brando's dick. Needless to say, he was rather upset.
(*JOHNSON appears from box*)
Ah, Johnson my friend, cocktails are served. Perhaps a bottle of Night Train or Tokay, then there's the cheap stuff.

JOHNSON

Mother, mother, mother, mother, MOTHER, MOTHER of MERCY, mother of the worms, mother of the worms, MOTHER OF MERCY, MOTHER OF WORMS AND LEGLESS THINGS, DON'T EVEN…

SAM
SHUT UP, HERE...Here you bastard.
(Gives him a hit/drink from bottle)

JOHNSON
I told them you want snakes. You want poison snakes. We got them. We got them. NO ARMS OR...

BABE
STOP FUCKIN' YELLING. (*BABE fake hits him*) Bam.

SAM
So it's a go. We do it. Paint the numbers, it's a fuckin' go. We do it, we go, we do it.

PROFESSOR
A fucking lift off.

ALLEY
We are self-employed.

SAM
Tomorrow.

JOHNSON
(Singing)
"There's no tomorrow, when love is true..."

(All singing "There's No Tomorrow")

BLACK OUT

Scene 3
SETTING: *The House.*
AT RISE: *MADGE and THOMAS*

THOMAS
Breakfast.

MADGE

Sausage, fat free.

THOMAS

Eggs.

MADGE

Passing through gauze.

THOMAS

Tire pressure.

MADGE

Thirty rear. Twenty-eight front.

THOMAS

Skin.

MADGE

Creamed.

THOMAS

Eyes.

MADGE

Searching.

THOMAS

Eyes.

MADGE

Focused.

THOMAS

Heart.

MADGE

Heart.

                        THOMAS
HEART!

                        MADGE
Breaking.

                        THOMAS
HEART!

                        MADGE
Counting.

                     (*LIGHTS FADE*)

Scene 4
SETTING: Train
AT RISE: MEN strap hanging, talking.

                        BABE
Why is everybody going the other way?

                        ALLEY
Queens, we're headed out, they're headed in.

                        JOHNSON
We forgot the fuckin' template. TEMPLATE! TEMPLE! I'M SORRY, MOMMA!

                        SAM
Johnson my friend, they have the template in Queens. We are going to make some money. Stencils.

                        PROFESSOR
She'll be wearing this ironed housedress that will have the scent of a hot iron on cotton.

                        BABE
What kind of store sells fuckin' templates? What the fuck is a template?

PROFESSOR

Template, temple, a layout for the perfect spiritual life, the fucking Godhead. Wake fucking up. Listen. Two of us will go in at first, to an art store, one will say, stencil, sir the stencil section. I will explain a certain yellow I need to complete my great work of jaundiced Rubens type women with swollen exploding nipples and you, my friend Babe, will do some stencil lifting. Slide the large numbered stencils into your trousers. I will complain about their small, meager selection of yellows, and I will say, I, like DaVinci, will be forced to make my own yellows, my own colors, true yellow, Gardenias. When I say, "my own colors", you are out of the store with the stencils. Alley, pay attention. You are the decoy, the man who looks like the thief, the rook about to take the queen, but Babe will be the pawn. A discovered mate.

JOHNSON

There is only one mother, the mother of love. The divine mother of truth. My mother died when she saw me on the tracks, the skids. I killed Mamma of a broken heart, listen…you fuckers…my Mamma's heart is broken…because of me…me…me…me…

BABE

Shut up Johnson. Do we have to take him, do we? Why, why, why…

PROFESSOR

Johnson is our soul. We are a gang, a fucking gang, a fucking men's group. We define our reality and he is in it.
(Turning)
Lady, you don't like the way I smell, get out of my way. Get out of this stinking subway. Johnson, I love you.
(Holding JOHNSON's face)
Is this a face? Is this a face?
(Kisses JOHNSON)
Look at this face. We're a gang on a train to Queens, on this train that smells like bad morning art piss. We are the realization of Sam's inspiration, numbers on a curb. We are self-employed. A work crew. A goddamn fellowship. CUT THE JUDGEMENT. JUST CUT IT!

BABE
YOU HEARD HIM, CUT THE FUCKIN' JUDGEMENT!
BLACKOUT

Scene 5
(LIGHTS fade up on house)

MADGE

Thomas, I'm going to need some cash today.

THOMAS

Cash.

MADGE

Yes.

THOMAS

I don't understand, cash?

MADGE

Spending money, loose change, to tip the boy who mows the lawn. The kids, for burgers and the school paper. Gas.

THOMAS

Gas goes on the card.

MADGE

Personal items, from the drug store.

THOMAS

They bill us.

MADGE

Personal items I don't want to show up on the bill. I need some cash, for Christ's sakes Thomas.

THOMAS

How much cash?

MADGE

Two hundred dollars. Pocket money, Thomas. Did you ever hear of pocket money?

(*LIGHTS OUT*)

Scene 6

(*LIGHTS fade up on Train*)

ALLEY

This is it, our stop. Let's go. Let's go, Babe. Hold the fuckin' door. We're off. We're in Queens. We made it, we fuckin' made it. Rego Park, a park, a fuckin' park, a fuckin' regal park of numbers. Hold it! We're getting off. BABE, HOLD THE FUCKIN' DOOR!

PROFESSOR

Gentlemen, let's paint some fucking numbers.

BLACKOUT

Scene 7

SETTING: The house
AT RISE: MADGE and THOMAS

THOMAS

Breakfast.

MADGE

Tofu pancakes.

THOMAS

Sex.

MADGE

Mutual morning masturbation. Over with. Thank God.

THOMAS

What did you say?

MADGE
Thank you for the pleasure you give me.

THOMAS
Children.

MADGE
Off to school.

THOMAS
House number.

MADGE
Nine, nine, nine.

THOMAS
I'm off to insure. Sir, Mr. Williams, when you die, unpleasant as the thought might be, do you want your loving wife and children to live in poverty, to give up all you've worked for? Mr. Williams, we can take care of them. We don't live forever. Prepare for the future or your nonfuture. Take care of your loved ones. Your tight knit little group of caring family, don't leave them with nothing. Safe Life will take care of them. We are after all, we are all human beings, for now.

MADGE
Nice presentation.

THOMAS
You think so?

MADGE
I know so. Have a wonderful day, Thomas.

THOMAS
Take care, dear.

(*LIGHTS fade*)

Scene 8

SETTING: Art Store
AT RISE: MEN and Salesman (MALCOLM)

PROFESSOR

It's a yellow I need, a jaundiced, liver yellow. The kind of yellow that makes grown men cry, the kind of yellow that turns night into morning, a spring insect yellow. The sun setting through the pollution of man's inability to identify his poison.

MALCOLM

Just a second, wait a second.

PROFESSOR

Sir, I have little time. I am in the middle of an important work of art.

MALCOLM

That man back there in the stencil section, the template stencil section, he looks like a shoplifter.

PROFESSOR

My dear sir, that man is my model, sir, he is a Golden Gloves champion, a specimen. I need a golden yellow, a golden glistening yellow, the yellow of champagne in the setting sun at Cannes, the yellow, the morning urine of genius, the yellow of cheap orange soda on a dry mouth morning, the yellow of candlelight reflected on one's first love. That man, he is no shoplifter, he is the soul of maleness.

MALCOLM

Yellow.

ALLEY

Listen, motherfucker, he wants yellow. Yellow! You want trouble?

PROFESSOR

A jaundiced, troubled, liver yellow. A desperate yellow. A Rubens yellow. A troubled mother's milk yellow.

MALCOLM

I'm going to have to call the manager.

PROFESSOR

My dear sir, many innocent people have died for the cause of art. You could be next, so I suggest you give us the yellow, the color of fear. I don't see that on your chart, your color wheel. Fear.

MALCOLM

That man back there...

PROFESSOR

Forget it. Pay attention.

MALCOLM

I have to call...

PROFESSOR
(*Rips phone out*)

No calls.

SAM

No fuckin' calls.

MALCOLM

He's putting stencils down his pants.

ALLEY

How's this down your pants?

SAM

You forget we were ever in here. Look at these fuckin' books. How to draw faces. How to draw flowers. How to draw animals. You prick, you sell these fuckin' books, you sell these books to kids who want to be artists, you prick.

PROFESSOR

I'm afraid the learned gentleman is correct.

SAM

Twelve bucks for these books? These books are bullshit. Twelve fuckin' rip-off bucks. How to draw flowers, how to draw a human face, a horse. How to draw a horse, you prick, you cruel bastard.

BABE
Kill him, fuckin' kill him! I'll draw your face all over the floor. I got the fuckin' stencils.

ALLEY
I got them too, the big ones. The good ones with the big numbers.

PROFESSOR
What is your name sir? So we know who we are doing business with.

MALCOLM
Malcolm.

JOHNSON
Pull his pants off so Mamma can see him.

MALCOLM
No. Please.

PROFESSOR
Malcolm, you sell these art books, these prints. The colors are totally untrue. The fucking colors are off. When Francis Bacon and I discussed the problem of reproduction, we realized that it is all the most humans get to see, reproductions of the truth. Do you know how unfortunate that is? Not unlike listening to the Brandenburgs on a three-inch torn speaker. How Bach would suffer. How much pain that would cause him, to miss so many notes, so many details…

JOHNSON
Take his pants off. Hey, pull them off…MALCOLM, LET MAMMA SEE.

MALCOLM
Just go, take what you want, please. PLEASE GO!

ALLEY
How to draw a human face, you prick, you mean fuckin' prick! Pull them.

JOHNSON
Look at his little shiny ass, no hair, like a woman.

MALCOLM
Please.

ALLEY
A human face, here's a small human face. (*Holding BABE's face*) Draw it.

PROFESSOR
DRAW IT! How to draw a flower, you can't, you can't. Here's the book up your bloody ass. Draw a flower, here draw it, draw it. DRAW IT. DRAW BABE'S FACE. IN MY HANDS, CAN'T YOU? LOOK AT THIS FACE! It says outside ART STORE! That my dear Malcolm, is a conflict of terms.

MALCOLM
I can't, CAN'T. I CAN'T DRAW. I CAN'T DRAW IT. LEAVE ME ALONE.

BABE
(*Kissing Malcolm*)
It's okay baby, you have a sweet mouth. OPEN IT! FUCKIN' OPEN IT!

MALCOLM
God, oh God.

PROFESSOR
We love you, Malcolm. Do you love us? You don't drink, do you Malcolm?

MALCOLM
No, sometimes with dinner.

ALLEY
You ever been in jail, Malcolm?

MALCOLM
No, never, and fuck you guys. You don't live in the real world. Big shots, screw you all.

SAM
Lay down on the floor, for art.

ALLEY
Open up sweet cheeks.

MALCOLM
Pricks.

SAM
Out of here, let's get out of here. Get the fuckin' paint, yellow.

ALLEY
SAY IT!

MALCOLM
I love you. I do. I really do.

BABE
You really do what.

MALCOLM
LOVE YOU.

ALLEY
Like brothers?

MALCOLM
YES. YES. YES.

SAM
Yes what?

MALCOLM
I LOVE YOU LIKE BROTHERS!

PROFESSOR
Malcolm, we love you too.

BABE
Don't ever forget us. Will you?

MALCOLM
Never.

PROFESSOR
Ta- ta, Malcom. Be a good boy. SAY IT!

MALCOLM
I love you. Ta-ta.

BABE
Ta-ta, he fuckin' said Ta-Ta.

MALCOLM
Ta, ta, TA, TA!

ALLEY
Stick the art books up his ass.

MALCOLM
Ta-TA!

PROFESSOR
How much do you love us?

MALCOLM
More than anything, I love you. Jesus.

PROFESSOR
One more thing Malcolm, why do you love us?

MALCOLM
You've given me no choice. God.

BABE
Good answer Malcolm. Fuck off.

(*MUSIC UP: "Unforgettable", Nat King Cole*)

Scene 9
SETTING: Front door. 999 Happiness Drive
AT RISE: MADGE and ESTHER

ESTHER
The thing is Madge, I go to the damn club, look, I mean how good can I look, sure it's not all physical, but the better I look the better I feel, and the better I feel the more I realize, who cares. Madge, you know, I mean, who cares, Madge you know what I mean?

MADGE
Yeah, sure I know.

ESTHER
They're creeps. Madge, are they? I mean maybe I should just talk for myself, Thomas is okay, you're getting along okay?

MADGE
Yeah, the same, you know, the same.

ESTHER
That's what I mean, the same, that's what I hate, the sameness. Madge, are we friends?

MADGE
Yeah, friends.

ESTHER
You know that medication is really screwing you up. I hate to say it but I feel like I've lost you.

MADGE
Esther, the mood swings were driving me crazy, did you want me to kill myself? Esther, I was feeling like killing myself. Now I'm on an even keel, no ups, no downs, even. What do I have to feel bad about, nothing.

ESTHER

Do you know how long we've been friends, neighbors, ten years, ten goddamn years honey, that's a long time. I hate to say it, are you listening honey, we are aging before each others eyes, day by day, minute by minute, where's the passion, are you gonna become a robot? Are we gonna become old sexless, metallic robots, shit! Are we Madge?

MADGE

I don't know, I don't know.

ESTHER

It's this place Madge, it's this damn place. I'm so sorry you're on those damn pills, they make you so, so cold, so indifferent. Come here, let's try, we can try, can we try? Can we? Madge? To goddamn feel?

MADGE

I don't know, I mean, yes, I want to, but my doctor said to try to stop, that's what he said, try to stop.

ESTHER

Try, try, try to stop having feelings. Is that what we do with our lives, try, try to stop? Is that it, a big goddamn stop sign, to passion, to love, what the hell are we protecting? Let's have a drink, let's smoke some pot, something. What are you protecting, what are you saving yourself for, for death, for the fucking prince devil?

MADGE

I don't know. I don't know. Maybe what I have is okay. My life is okay.

ESTHER

OKAY, okay, is that good enough? OKAY, FUCK OKAY, that's okay for you? OKAY. Come here, come here, feel your skin Madge, is that okay, is it?

MADGE

It feels good.

ESTHER

How good?

MADGE

Really good.

ESTHER

You should get off the damn pills, baby you really should. They make you cold.

MADGE

I should do a lot of things.

ESTHER

Let's make a pact, honey, to try new things, to have a little goddamn fun, to not get sucked in, that's what they do, Billy-boy, Thomas-boy, they sucked us in, fucked up our potential for pleasure, what do you say, try new things, the clock is ticking.

MADGE

Sure Esther, thanks, you're a good friend…

ESTHER

We need to feel good, you understand, through the fucking medication honey, without pleasure there's nothing. Come here.

MADGE

Jesus Esther, you feel so good.

ESTHER

Because I'm alive, because you're alive, that's all we have baby, what's in front of us.

MADGE

We'll run a hot bath, full of bubbles…My shrink said…

ESTHER

And drink some wine.
(THEY embrace. KNOCK at door.)
Who the hell could that be?

MADGE
I'll see who it is.

ESTHER
Don't get it, screw them. Let's just spend the afternoon together, you and me...

MADGE
Yeah, okay, you and me. I'll try Esther.
(*More knocking*)
Jesus.
(*Going to door*)
Yes, can I help you?

SAM
Your number is done ma'am. 9-9-9, pretty as a picture. That's twenty dollars, cash.

MADGE
What number?

ALLEY
The sidewalk number ma'am – your house number painted on the curb.

MADGE
We didn't ask for any number on that curb.

ESTHER
Who is it?

MADGE
It's a bunch of bums.

SAM
Lady, it's on all the curbs. The whole neighborhood has them. Twenty bucks.

MADGE
I have no cash.

SAM
Lady, we're not looking for grief. Twenty bucks…

MADGE
We didn't ask for any numbers, so thank you very…

PROFESSOR
Madame, my name is Stuart Applebaum. I'm the street manager and you are…?

MADGE
Madge. Mrs. Roberts. Madge Roberts.

PROFESSOR
Well Madge, unpleasant as it might be, the curb numbers are a fact of life. You are, you seem to be, an intelligent, attractive woman. Numbers are a fact of life. You understand facts of life?

MADGE
Mr…

PROFESSOR
Applebaum, like the tree, apples. My road gang and myself are honest, hard working men.

ESTHER
Who is it?

MADGE
A road gang, some sort of…you're English, from England?

PROFESSOR
Very perceptive, yes, English from England.

MADGE
I love how you people speak, so formal, so homosexual.

PROFESSOR

Well, Madge or Meg or Mary, that's very perceptive. We need our twenty dollars or would you like a cock up your ass – from a British faggot?
(*PAUSE*)

MADGE

Mr...what was it?

PROFESSOR

Applebaum. Like the tree and the lip treatment. Apple-Baum, the lips and the tree.

ESTHER

(*Coming to door*)

Jesus! Who are they honey?

MADGE

Painters, numbers, number men. We're busy now, come back later.

PROFESSOR

My dear, sweet woman, there is no later. Twenty dollars for the number. Cash.

ESTHER

Madge, invite them in.

MADGE

Jesus, Esther.

ESTHER

Come on. We'll have some fun. Ask them in.

MADGE

Well, I've heard you people like your tea. Would you like some tea, iced if you like? I have one called English Breakfast tea and other herbal teas.

PROFESSOR

My men are painters, numbers, we're doing the neighborhood. MEN! How about a tea break? Such hard workers they are.

MADGE
Come in Mr. Applebaum, into my home. I don't know about…

PROFESSOR
And our contingent of workers, see we are all equal, the same, none better, none worse. We are self-employed, Madge. Socialists. Social people.

MADGE
There won't be any trouble.

PROFESSOR
The last thing we want is trouble.

ALLEY
You son of a bitch, you're fuckin' amazing.

MADGE
Come in gentlemen. Now, Mr…

PROFESSOR
Stuart.

ESTHER
So you gentlemen are painters, number painters.

PROFESSOR
Quite right.
(*The MEN all agree*)

ESTHER
That must be an interesting line of work. There's no limit to numbers.

MADGE
Oh, this is Esther. You see. Stuart, it is Stuart?

PROFESSOR
That's very good, yes, Stuart.

MADGE

You see Stuart, my husband and I were thinking of painting the bedroom, we thought black, a black bedroom. It was my idea, black. Black like a darkroom, a room of development. Maybe you'd like to give us, Thomas and I, an estimate on painting the bedroom. You men are painters.

PROFESSOR

Yes we are, highly skilled professionals.

MADGE

The white bedroom, making it black, black over white. Better weekend mornings, don't you think? Black over white, how many coats?

PROFESSOR

Mrs…

MADGE

Roberts…do the men want tea?

PROFESSOR

Men, tea?

(*MEN say: Tea…I hate fuckin' tea, You crazy?…Jesus…etc.*)

PROFESSOR

Miz Roberts, do you have beer, I sense the men would prefer it…

MADGE

Well, I don't know about…

PROFESSOR

Black! A room of black love…endangered love, black, dark love and sex.

MADGE

Yes, Mr.?

(*MEN looking ESTHER over*)

PROFESSOR

Call me Stuart.

MADGE
You seem like a sensitive man.

PROFESSOR
And you, my dear Mrs. Roberts, keep a very orderly house, everything in place. Now, for example, I always misplace my car keys.

MADGE
Our keys are here, all alphabetized. Here's the A; Audi, B; Buick, V; Volvo. Nothing Japanese, we don't drive anything from Japan. And the one for the ancient Volkswagen, '71 convertible, blue, left out to rot.

PROFESSOR
You must have a very clever husband. Old, blue, rotten Volkswagen convertibles are wise investments.

MADGE
He's bright. Yes, he's bright, Thomas is. Let me show you the bedroom and how badly it needs a paint job and other work done. They won't hurt her?

PROFESSOR
I can assure you, these men are gentlemen. Appearances are often deceiving.

SAM
Hey Professor, lets get the fuck out of here, let's go, let's get out of here.

ALLEY
It's bad fuckin' decorating, bad taste.

PROFESSOR
Relax Madge, these men are laborers, they've had a tough time of it, their hearts are filled with compassion and love because of their suffering, they're good people, tough but honest.

MADGE
I don't want to be raped, not gang raped, by number painters.

PROFESSOR

My dear Madge, the only crime these men have committed is that of failure, not living up to their fucking mother's expectations.

MADGE

I've invited you in for tea. Tea.

PROFESSOR

Iced-cold-tea. That relaxes the tongue. Steaming-hot tea, that warms and moistens the loins.

MADGE

Listen…

PROFESSOR

Stuart.

MADGE
(*Pulling him downstage*)

Stuart, listen Stuart, you want me to strip okay, okay, just don't gang rape me. I'll strip okay. OKAY? You want to see my breasts okay, just don't hurt me. I need you to be gentle, at the beginning, that's all it's been for me is beginnings, no endings, nothing final, look I'm showing you, look, you want to see the rest, do you, the flesh, here, just don't gang rape me, don't make me afraid. Stuart, I'm a mother, Stuart, that's your name…Stuart…

PROFESSOR

Right. Stuart. Madge, you are a very sweet and attractive woman, you don't need to over dramatize, I think black is a good choice, for the BEDROOM, nonreflective, black EATS all the other colors.
(*To ALLEY*)
Get the car keys. The Volvo wagon.

MADGE

So you won't hurt me.

PROFESSOR
Why, sweet lady, in God's name would we hurt you?

MADGE
Tell me your name again.

PROFESSOR
Stuart.

MADGE
Stuart, we can be personal, you and I, can be private.

PROFESSOR
You do enjoy the hot iron on the cotton, the lack of folds, wrinkles.

MADGE
Listen Stuart, it is Stuart, between you and me, you seem like a lover. You'll need to kiss me. And be gentle. In the hands, in the hands. A soft touch. Then go, and that's all, then the bedroom is black, no paint needed.

PROFESSOR
Paintless, painless.

MADGE
You have beautiful lips.

ALLEY
There's nothing here, let's go.

BABE
Let's do her.

SAM
Let's go.

PROFESSOR
Gentlemen, I think I'm falling in love.
   (*Begins singing "Falling in Love with Love"*)

MADGE
Stuart, don't hurt me, don't hurt Esther.

(*MEN coming on with ESTHER*)

ESTHER
GET AWAY FROM ME!

PROFESSOR
GENTLEMEN! Cool and fucking calm. Dear friends, let's all relax.
(*To ESTHER*)
My dear lady, no one will so much as harm a hair on your beautiful head.

ALLEY
She'll call the cops, this one.

MADGE
No, no I won't.
(*To Stuart*)
Stay with me, it's okay, stay with me.
(*To MEN*)
There's booze downstairs, in the oak cabinet, lots of it.
(*To Stuart*)
I have this skin, that gives me this pain, be gentle, that's all I ask, gentleness.

ALLEY
This number shit was a bad idea.

JOHNSON
I want to go back. MOMMA! BACK! BACK! BACK! MOMMA, I'M SORRY.

MADGE
Stuart, you make me so hot, like a fire.

ALLEY
There is nothing to take, just crap. Glasses and books, fuckin' books all over the place. This place is a fuckin' library. How to do this. How to do fuckin' that. Time-Life How to fix everything.

SAM
I found pills, downs, ups, everything. The fuckin' medicine chest is full, here Babe, Alley, Johnson, here Professor, fuckin' pills.

MADGE
No, don't take the pills, just don't take my medication. PLEASE!

ESTHER
Let them take it, Madge, GOOD FUCKING RIDDANCE.

ALLEY
(Like a rap song)
It says Prozac, Pro-fuckin'-zack, Val-fuckin'-Yum, Lib-fuckin'-Bre-Um, Co-fuckin'-Dean, Meth-a-fuckin'-drean, Meth-a-fuckin'-done, Seca-fuckin'-all, Tuna-fuckin'-all! All, all, all…

MADGE
ESTHER! ESTHER! MY MEDICATION! ESTHER DON'T LET THEM TAKE MY MEDICATION…listen, we'll have a party. A party, don't take my pills. Babe! Leave my pills. ESTHER!

ESTHER
GOOD RIDDANCE, MADGE. THANK GOD!

PROFESSOR
We'll all take them darling. We'll swallow them all, like goddamn fucking whales sucking plankton in the sea.

MADGE
Babe, don't take them. What does that tattoo say, "Eat Shit"? Babe, that is beautiful, so to the point. Babe's tattoo says "Eat Shit" on the bicep. Have you boys ever eaten shit? I have, I really have. For years… for years…

PROFESSOR
Dear Madge. I think, therefore I am! I think there…

MADGE
For God's sake don't think. This place reeks of thinking. Look at the

MADGE, continued
napkin drawer; the forks, dessert spoons, look, everything in place. I got out, because I was cute, sexy, pretty. I did not want this life, you guys are trouble, have some tea. "Sleepytime", herbal, here's one, "Down Time", here's one, "Waste Of Time", another tea, "LONG LIFE, NO FUN". Here's one called "FUCK EVERYTHING...FUCK EVERYTHING...my medication...

ESTHER
It's okay, honey.

PROFESSOR
SHUT UP, SHUT UP...I THINK THEREFORE I AM!

SAM
Let's get back to work, the curbs, numbers. Let's make some goddamn money...

PROFESSOR
Let's go, gentlemen. Numbers on the fucking curbs, our labor of love. Farewell ladies! A toast to...the acoustics of reality...
(*Sounds of sirens*)

SAM
Fuck.

ALLEY
Fuck, lady...

MADGE
I didn't call. I swear, I didn't call them.

PROFESSOR
Our lost love Malcolm, that's who fucking called.

ALLEY
You know what you are ladies, hostages. You are pieces of ass hostages.

JOHNSON
The buzz men.

BABE
We didn't do anything, she invited us in, didn't you? Didn't you?

MADGE
I love you all, we are having a party, a little party, a little…

(*DETECTIVE'S VOICE from outside*)

DETECTIVE'S VOICE
YOU ARE SURROUNDED! JUST WALK OUT THE DOOR WITH YOUR HANDS OVER YOUR HEADS AND NOBODY WILL GET HURT!

ALLEY
Queens, we had to come to fuckin' Queens.

SAM
Shit, we were doin' great, just paintin' numbers.

DETECTIVE'S VOICE
(*From outside*)
LET THE WOMEN OUT.

MADGE
WE ARE HAVING A PARTY. GET AWAY FROM MY HOME.

DETECTIVE'S VOICE
LET THEM OUT.

THOMAS' VOICE
MADGE, ARE YOU OKAY?

MADGE
Jesus, it's Thomas.

ESTHER
SHE'S FINE. WE ARE BOTH FINE.

MADGE
I'M FINE. GO AWAY.

THOMAS
HONEY...I LOVE... YOU...

MADGE
FUCK OFF, THOMAS.

DETECTIVE'S VOICE
LADIES, THESE MEN ARE DANGEROUS.

ALLEY
Fuckin' sweet ass Malcom, we should have killed him.

DETECTIVE'S VOICE
LET THE WOMEN OUT! THIS IS YOUR LAST CHANCE!

MADGE
WE ARE CELEBRATING, YOU JERKS! WE ARE HAVING A TEA PARTY.

DETECTIVE'S VOICE
WE'RE GONNA THROW TEAR GAS IN.

PROFESSOR
We need some fucking cocktails.

JOHNSON
I'm scared. MOMMA, DON'T HURT ME, DON'T...

DETECTIVE'S VOICE
YOU HAVE SIXTY SECONDS...

JOHNSON
I'M COMING OUT. DON'T SHOOT. AMNESTY, ATTICA. I'M COMING OUT...ATTICA...

ESTHER
Have a drink Johnson. Calm down, nobody is shooting anybody.

JOHNSON
MOMMA, MOMMA I'M SORRY, MOMMA, I'M SORRY...
(*JOHNSON runs out, sound of shots*)

MADGE
BASTARDS!

ESTHER
ASSHOLES!

PROFESSOR
He's bloody hit, he's shot. WE ARE ALL FUCKING BROTHERS AND SISTERS! FUCKING ANIMALS!
(*More shots*)

MADGE
WE ARE GETTING AN ESTIMATE ON A PAINT JOB!

ESTHER
WE PAY YOU. YOU'RE OUR PAID SERVANTS. YOU ASSHOLES...

MADGE
BASTARDS, CREEPS...

JOHNSON
(*Crawling in, bleeding*)
Oh momma, oh momma, mommy, momma...don't hurt me...I'm sorry...

MADGE
Put him in the bathtub, Jesus! Poor thing, upstairs, the carpet's ruined, Jesus...

ESTHER
Oh God, oh God...

(*ALLEY, BABE, SAM help him up.*)
(*JOHNSON and SAM exit.*)

DETECTIVE'S VOICE
THIS IS DETECTIVE SHIELDS. I'M COMING IN. I AM NOT ARMED. I AM NOT ARMED. I REPEAT, I AM NOT ARMED. I'M COMING IN.

(*Enters pointing GUN*)

Hello, I'm Detective…IT'S OKAY MEN, I'M IN, I'm Detective Shields. Okay everyone, cool and calm, just cool and calm, cool and calm, everyone cool and calm. COOL AND CALM!

(*PROFESSOR gracefully walks up to him and takes the GUN away*)

PROFESSOR
Listen your honor, your detectiveship, we haven't done a thing. We are trying to make an honest living. Certainly you can see that. Numbers.

DETECTIVE
Let the women out.

MADGE
We don't want to go out. This is my home, sir, and you are intruding on a friendly gathering. I've seen Waco on TV. I've seen the way you bastards operate. Can I, can I kick him in the balls? Waco, you prick.

ESTHER
She's right. Waco, you prick.

DETECTIVE
I have a wife that makes you look, lady, like a train wreck.

PROFESSOR
How dare you insult these ladies. HOW DARE YOU! If I may say so sir, you watch too many bad movies. Many of which I have, some years ago, appeared in. We are men plagued with guilt, easily transformed to anger. THEN HATE.

DETECTIVE
What's your relationship to these women? (*ALLEY and BABE enter*)

ALLEY

Let's kill this fuckin' guy.

BABE

Yeah, what the fuck.

DETECTIVE

I suggest you men stop drinking.

PROFESSOR

That, my friend is a very bad idea. Our relationship is that of fellow human beings, number painters and paintees. And fucking workers of the TRUTH! And we will drink and do what ever the fucking hell we want.

MADGE

So why don't you leave officer, and take Mr. Johnson to the hospital. The man is bleeding to death in our tub, my tub of love, my love tub.

DETECTIVE

I suggest you return my revolver.

PROFESSOR

That is a very bad suggestion, how about a bullet up your fucking ass.

MADGE

Why don't you and your so-called men get away from here. You wait, you wait till our congressman hears about this.

ESTHER

He happens to be my brother-in-law.

MADGE

Thank you Esther, my neighbor Esther, Esther with the beautiful breasts and ass. Esther and I shower together, while the men are off, something you weakling punks dream about.

ESTHER

Should I call him right now, Congressman Flanders, ever hear of him?

BABE
(*Entering*)

Let me break his fuckin' face.

ESTHER

It's okay Babe, not yet.

DETECTIVE

You're Babe Basho, the fighter. I saw you fight. Jesus, what happened to you? You were the best.

BABE

I'll break your fuckin' head open. What happened to me, what happened to me, what happened to me? I'll show you what happened to me!

ALLEY

It's okay, Babe.

DETECTIVE

Jesus, you were good, really good. Lots of flash and you could deliver. Fast and powerful. Babe Basho, Jesus.

PROFESSOR

It seems sir, your detectiveship, we have a situation here. We don't want any trouble.

DETECTIVE

The place is surrounded, it's gonna be bad. You'll be killed, all of you. Sharpshooters and everything.

PROFESSOR

Are you a chess player, Detective Shields?

DETECTIVE

A chess player, no wait...WAIT! I saw you in that movie with what's his name, the one about the wife...with what's his name, it was on last night...what's his name...?

PROFESSOR
His name was George Sanders…he killed himself, dear George did. His suicide note read, "I'm bored." George was too intelligent for his own good, an excellent chess player.

MADGE
He's a movie star, I knew it. I knew it. I knew it the minute I saw him.

PROFESSOR
My dear, I wore a suit that cost more than this badly decorated house, but you my dear are such an attractive woman. How much I want you.
(*Singing*)
"Falling in love with love is falling for…"

SAM
(*Entering*)
He's bleedin' to death, Johnson's almost dead. The tub is fillin' up with blood.

DETECTIVE
FUCK, it'll be on the goddamn news.
(*Clearing his throat*)

DETECTIVE
We're interested in the truth, you give up now and it's over with. Or you guys are gonna be shot down like pigs and turned into bacon.

MADGE
I'm going to leave my husband, it's true. I'm leaving Thomas.

ESTHER
Madge. We'll do it together.

MADGE
I am. I mean it Esther…

ESTHER
God bless you Madge, and fuck Billy-boy too.

PROFESSOR

God fucking bless you Madge and beautiful Esther too.

DETECTIVE

You guys are fucked, you know that, you're gonna die, like pigs. White pigs. Slammed.

BABE

Make him fuckin' crawl.

DETECTIVE

There is no way out.

ALLEY

Stick the gun up his ass and blow him fuckin' away. We get in the Volvo with the babes and…fly…

PROFESSOR

It's a slow automobile, no pick up. Overpriced, for the over-safe. When James Dean and I raced to the liquor store, him, in his beat up Porsche, listening to the tapes of Kerouac…I said, I SAID! DEAR JAMES, ACTING, ACTING, acting, is like a woman undressing behind a screen – almost transparent, his sweet lips on my absent mouth… sweet James…STAY IN FUCKING CONTROL…I made it…passed him on the way back…in his fucking wreck…me going back to the party in my XKE or was it the fucking MG, who fucking knows. BUT! I could not stop for James, sweet James…sweet…

DETECTIVE

I got a deal for you; the women go out, I'll stay, we leave together. I call the squad cars and choppers off, we'll drive to Mexico or Canada or wherever you want and that's the end of it. We drop your friend off at the hospital.

ALLEY

Let's fuckin' kill him.

BABE
Let's kill him. Let me fuckin' kill him. He's full of shit. I'll beat his fuckin' head in.

SAM
He's gone, Johnson is dead, he's dead. Gimme a goddamn drink, fuckin' numbers. He looks okay all red and all. Kill this bastard. He didn't do a fuckin' thing. He's got a smile on his face, Johnson does, no shit, a smile and a hard-on like a fuckin' elephant. Oh yeah, he took his pants off in his blood, imagine, in his blood, it's beautiful. Ladies please, do it to him, he's warm, he's warm, send him to eternal heaven.

MADGE
Please no, please. Please.

ESTHER
Oh what the hell, Madge.

MADGE
Esther, Jesus.

ESTHER
What the hell Madge? Don't you understand, don't you understand? Like a sunset, an elephant. Let's love him, finish him while they kill this bastard. Let's get up there in the tub and send him to heaven. Madge listen, he could have been a poet, a poet who lost his brains. They all do. It's so sad, so sad. It wasn't his fault. It wasn't Sammy's fault. It's the least we can do. It's something Madge, it's doing something for goodness.

PROFESSOR
THANK YOU, THANK YOU FOR GOD! FOR GOD AND ALL THE EVILNESS HE CREATES.

MADGE
For all the evilness he creates.

(WOMEN EXIT)
MUSIC UP (TIBETAN MONKS chanting, MEN arm in arm rocking)

PROFESSOR
FOR LOVE, FOR GODDAMN LOVE…

(*BABE beats the DETECTIVE, MEN surround BABE and DETECTIVE, WOMEN come back and join ritual*)

MADGE
I never made love to a dead man.

ESTHER
The hot blood, the endless hard-on, endlessness, endless…

PROFESSOR
Alley, get the car.
(*Yelling out the door*)
WE ARE DRIVING OUT OF HERE. YOU GET OUT OF THE FUCKING WAY. WE HAVE YOUR DETECTIVE SHIELDS AND THE LADIES AND THE WORLD BY THE BALLS. AND WE DON'T GIVE A FUCKING SHIT WHO OR WHAT LIVES OR DIES.
(*Coming down stage BABE and PROFESSOR*)

BABE
I could fight in Mexico.

PROFESSOR
You could fight the brave bulls, in Mexico.

BABE
I've got the, what do you call them…?
PROFESSOR
Stencils…

BABE
I've got them in my pants, are numbers the same in Mexico, in case we need work?…in my pants, inside my underwear against me, the numbers…I'm in one of the numbers. It could be zero. It could be six. It could be eight, it could be…ten…round…open…sixteen…in my pants…

(*ALL EXIT. FADE*)
(*MUSIC UP*)
(*Sound of car driving off*)

Scene 10
SETTING: *House*
AT RISE: *JOHNSON on stage, a ghost. He's covered with blood stained fabric. THOMAS enters.*

THOMAS
Madge? Madge? MADGE?

JOHNSON
Mamma's gone.

THOMAS
(*Rubbing eyes, never seeing JOHNSON*)
Madge, come on now. Dinner time. I'm home.

JOHNSON
Gone.

THOMAS
Kids, Daddy's home. Kiss goodnight.

JOHNSON
Mexico, Mamma, Mexico.

THOMAS
Madge, I'm getting angry. It's not funny. Dinner.

JOHNSON
Lobster, boiled.

THOMAS
Vegetable.

JOHNSON
Beet.

THOMAS
Madge? MADGE! SEX!

JOHNSON
Blood tub.

THOMAS
I have a surprise for you and the kids. Madge?

JOHNSON
Mamma's gone. Babies gone.

THOMAS
Four policies, I had my best day. Dinner Madge. Where's the Volvo?

JOHNSON
Death fuck.

THOMAS
Are you in the shower? It's six-thirty. Your shower should be over.

JOHNSON
All over.

THOMAS
I've brought you a surprise. I've spent money on a pie, an apple pie for you, Madge. Madge? Lip balm, for your chapped, un-kissed lips. Madge, it's time we kissed. Four policies, imagine.

JOHNSON
Mamma goes, everything goes.

THOMAS
Madge?

(*LIGHTS fade, MUSIC up*)
(End of ACT I)

ACT II

Scene 1

SETTING: Mexican beach at dusk
AT RISE: The MEN have beach gear and scuba stuff,
ESTHER in beach wear.

ALLEY

Jesus, Mexico, it's beautiful.

BABE

We got it all. We got it all.

ALLEY

Mexico, hotel rooms, scuba gear, tequila, not freezing our balls off in New York. Too bad Johnson's not here.

BABE

Yeah, fuckin' Johnson, Jesus, I miss him.

ALLEY

Come on Babe, hey Professor, we'll spear some fuckin' sea life.

BABE

He wanted to start a business with us.

ALLEY

Come on man, let's have some fun.

BABE

I don't know how, okay? My mother never taught me how, okay. OKAY! OKAY! OKAY! OKAY, YOU FUCKERS!

PROFESSOR

Gentlemen, gentlemen, gentlemen, I think we need separation. As my nurse would say, Stuart darling, you need some time alone.

ALLEY
Yeah, did she wipe your ass too?

PROFESSOR
As a matter of fact she did.

ALLEY
Did she jerk you off?

PROFESSOR
As a matter of fact, yes she did – with quite the experience.

ALLEY
You see, you had all the advantages.

BABE
That's why he talks like that.

PROFESSOR
Ah yes my friends, but I was quite unloved. Nursie was but a paid, whoring, ass-wiping slut.

BABE
HEY! HEY!

ESTHER
Join the losers to be a winner, charming and wonderful and brilliant.

BABE
Yeah Esther.

ALLEY
A toast to Esther.

ESTHER
Do you know why I love you, love you all? Alley? Babe? The late Johnson? Stuart…because you're? Come on…come on words…

ALLEY

Hopeless.

BABE

Fucked up.

ALLEY

Losers.

BABE

Champs.

ALLEY

Handsome, sexy, big shots.

BABE

Well built, well hung.

ALLEY

Piss bum killers.

BABE

Powerful, fearless.

ALLEY

Filled with fear, semi-dramatic drunks.

ESTHER

When I killed that guy, where was it? San Antonio, in Texas, that was a lesson, a lesson in the frailty of human life. See, he was a guy who was done. I saw it in his eyes. His sex was dead. Now, unless you are either a genius, a fucking poet-artist or a drunk, slash, criminal – present company excluded of course – when your sex is dead, you are dead. So killing a dead man is not killing. It is forgiving.

BABE

Forgiving, not killing.

ESTHER
I cannot fuck my way into heaven or steal my way into heaven or suck my way into heaven. Wake up fuckers! YOU WORLD, HAVE PLAYED GAMES, the question is...does...

ALLEY
Cool out Esther.

ESTHER
THE QUESTION IS...DOES...

BABE
I'm the fuckin' champ, that's who...that's who.

ESTHER
DOES THE BRAIN, THE MIND, LIVE ON? DO THE THOUGHTS LIVE ON AFTER DEATH? THAT'S THE QUESTION!

BABE
That's who...THAT'S WHO!

ESTHER
OF COURSE IT DOES. THE MIND LIVES ON. When I killed that guy, I killed him...it felt...it felt...great.

ALLEY
Have a drink, Esther.

ESTHER
I can't. Okay, I can't. I try but I can't, I can't. My stomach can't take it. I am not one of you. I want to be, but I'm not one of you. Do you still have eyes? Pricks, do you have eyes? Are you eyeless snakes?

PROFESSOR
We love you like an Egyptian sunrise, dear Esther.

ALLEY

I love you, Esther.

BABE

Esther's my girl.

ESTHER

Yeah, well too bad, I don't know if I love you. So fuck off boys. Rejection is a tough nail to bite. It hurts the teeth.

ALLEY

You know what, Esther? You're fuckin' dead. We should have never brought you.

ESTHER

Oh, aren't you the tough boys! Impotent, the alcohol has made you ball-less. Not a hard cock amongst you. Delusion! Illusion!

ALLEY

Kill her.

BABE

NO! Don't you hurt her.

ESTHER

OOOOH (*singing*) the window she is broken and the rain, she is coming in…Mañana…

ALLEY

Bitch…

ESTHER

Losers, losers, leeches of the earth. Why did God make you? To suck on bottles, like babies, like sexless nothings…you call this fun?

ALLEY

Do her Babe, do her, like she did for Johnson. Do it Babe.

BABE

Get off my back. Don't ever tell me what to do. I CAN'T, OKAY. I CAN'T! MY MOTHER NEVER TAUGHT ME HOW!

ALLEY

You can't, you fucker. You can't.

ESTHER

He can't. It's okay.

ALLEY

She's a dead man.

BABE

How could a woman be a dead man?

ESTHER
(*Singing*)

Oh the car she cannot start, and the man he is broken, the waves beat on the dock…but…Man…

BABE

Yeah Esther! Yeah!

ESTHER

Am I your babe, your babe, your babe, the babe of the losers beautiful? What we are going to do…is…is climb those cliffs and float down, look at that night flying egret, look. One…beautiful…moment of flight…one perfect moment…Mexican air in the nostrils…then smash…it's everything. You see that, Alley, Babe?

ALLEY

I don't know…

ESTHER

Listen, that few seconds will seem longer than everything, your whole lives, you will be the perfect Olympic divers.

ALLEY
I don't know…it sounds weird…we're not divers. You're asking us to kill ourselves. Is that it Esther?

BABE
Jesus.

ESTHER
Alley, how many times have you been in detox?

ALLEY
Fifty, a hundred, I don't know, I don't know. Someplace, somehow I got screwed.

ESTHER
Screwed.

ALLEY
Yeah, it all went wrong, something got fucked. Went wrong I mean…

ESTHER
You like me Alley?

ALLEY
Yeah, I like you…

ESTHER
Well, that's beautiful. Alley, it's you and me. You could get a car dealership – Ford, Toyota. I'm not too old to have kids. What do you think?

ALLEY
You mean it, Esther?

ESTHER
Absolutely.

ALLEY
Me and you and forget this stuff?

ESTHER
No more getting high. No more drinking. Babe, how many times have you been in detox?

BABE
Over a hundred.

ESTHER
And you know what? You drive great. You know what? I waited my whole life for you guys. Feel your legs, feel the power, we climb, we dive. Babe lock in, Babe, lock in, BABE! You lost okay, big deal. You lost.

BABE
I could have won, son of a bitch. I could have won, one punch.

ESTHER
We all could have won. We still can. That's the great thing.

ALLEY
Esther, Esther, you mean it, about you and me and the car dealership?

ESTHER
Of course I mean it, maybe, sometime, someday.

BABE
You first Esther, climb the cliffs.

ESTHER
So you can look at my ass?

ALLEY
Yeah, so we can look at your ass.

ESTHER
So you have some esthetic to follow.

BABE
What does that mean, esthetic?

ALLEY
It means nice ass. We die for Esther's nice ass.

BABE
Christ died for our sins, my mother told me that.

ALLEY
We die for Esther's ass. I don't see the big difference.

ESTHER
We are going to hit the warm sea and be cleansed. There won't be any dying, only rebirth. The trick is to keep the arms in front to break the fall, to cut the water. Then it doesn't break your heads. You don't want your heads to break, do you?

ALLEY
You're saying, the thing to remember is to keep your arms out.

ESTHER
Keep the arms out.

BABE
The head, protect the head. The brain.

ESTHER
Follow me up. To heaven.

ALLEY
Her ass is so perfect. It's like this…this vertical smile.

BABE
The ass of God.

ALLEY
WE are the fuckin' apostles of the ass of God.

BABE
The ass of God.

ALLEY
Apostles of the ass of God.

Scene 2

SETTING: Two months later, a beach in Mexico
AT RISE: PROFESSOR and MADGE on the beach Him singing "Talk to the Animals"

PROFESSOR
Madge darling, if it wouldn't be too much trouble, some more tequila.

MADGE
I'm bored.

PROFESSOR
Make love to some more beach boys.

MADGE
I'm bored. They hurt. Not really there, not interesting. Trying to win some contest. That big boy on the beach over there is the worst. He'll never get off the island. He eats fish and rides the horses, hooves on the night beach.

PROFESSOR
Enjoy your own mind and the creatures of the sea.

MADGE
Do you love me?

PROFESSOR
Madge, I love…I find your middle classness incredibly sexy, all the details of your body like the Mexican clouds in motion, ripples with the underwater sandscapes of random sex.

MADGE
Do you always have to be drunk?

PROFESSOR
My sweet Madge, I am never and always drunk. If you want to go back you can. Look at Babe with the beautiful Mexican woman and Alley and Sam in the sea, like fish. I have never seen them smile before. And your children speaking fluent Spanish, all tan and blond.

MADGE
You really don't mind that I make love to the big, black man on the white horse with the pounding hooves?

PROFESSOR
Life was made to have visions, to transcend. No Madge, I don't mind.

MADGE
And the woman, the hotel baker with the dark hair, who you play chess with all night. The way her breasts hang over the board, it must affect your mind. I watch from the terrace, her beautiful nipples in the moonlight, it must affect your game. The star feature of your mind, it must affect your thought process, how the moves are made, her extended nipples on the chessboard.

PROFESSOR
Her nipples on the chessboard are not unlike Detective Shields back in Rego Park begging for his life as Babe bashed his head in. Nipples have an odd place in a chess game, in the rational mind, the mind of sex, the mind of rational thought, of love.

MADGE
Are her nipples...are they more beautiful than mine in the Mexican moonlight, over a chessboard?

PROFESSOR
My dear Madge, life is not a nipple beauty contest, elongated nipples on a board, when we drove out of Queens, in that awful, slow Volvo and I saw the sweet look on your face, and the children's faces, leaving the Montessori school, you a school girl cutting class and that tear of freedom and the way you must have made love to Johnson in the tub of blood, and stealing car after car and the look on your face, skin getting

PROFESSOR, continued

tighter and your white teeth so brave and that last terrible holdup, with the fear and the unforgivable killing to get us here on this Mexican beach. I can still see the fear in your beautiful eyes and the short history of our love.

MADGE

It's the drunkenness, please, it's not the killing. It's the drunkenness and getting away with it, the confusion. When do we pay? Stuart, when do we pay? God, it's so evil, your nipple chess game.

PROFESSOR

Discovered mate, look at that moon, Madge, look at that goddamn moon. Isn't that something? And the music of the waves, isn't that something? And your children playing games with stones and shells with the Mexican kids, with no clock ticking.

MADGE

It is something.
(Pause)
Don't you miss acting, the movies? It's not too late Stuart, isn't enough enough? Bottle after bottle, my God. How far can you push it?

PROFESSOR

Enough is most certainly not enough. BABE, THAT WAS A MOST BEAUTIFUL DIVE. Did you see the way he split the reflection of the moon and made it shimmer? Dear Madge, you take it all so seriously. Everything is so beautiful just the way it is, just the way it is. You are beautiful, just the way it is, for God's sake, let it be. Didn't one of the Beatles say that?

MADGE

Paul McCartney or George Harrison, it's a song, *Let It Be*.

PROFESSOR

No relation to Rex, Rex said to me, Stuart, you are a wonderful talent, but...Alley, Sam, that was wonderful, the configuration of them and Esther and the two Mexican women standing, falling, standing, falling, so pedestrian in its grace, so un-choreographed. So fucking

PROFESSOR, continued

unrehearsed. You know Burton gave me this great blow job while Liz was asleep and he looked up and said, imagine, "Don't tell Liz", in that voice of his, "Don't tell Liz." Then he passed out and there she was; the silk sheet down past her stomach and thighs, the clump of sweet black hair. The classic mouth, Richard, my friend on the floor, smiling, so I climbed up on Liz, like the fucking Titanic. She never awakened, no sign of life, but we did it, fucking Liz and I. She did kiss back, in her stupor, this sweet baby kiss, such soft lips. In the morning Richard and I had this huge breakfast, champagne and a seafood omelet. Richard, in that voice said, "Mornings are the introduction to hell." Liz came to breakfast in this see-through thing, her nipples still hard. I could see the embarrassment on Richard's face, as he elegantly, brilliantly poured the morning coffee, with only a slight tremor of hand, as he kissed Liz on her soft morning neck, but…

MADGE

But what?

PROFESSOR

But what indeed.

MADGE

Rex Harrison, what did he say, Stuart?

PROFESSOR

I said, see, it's not what Rex said, the big queen, but what I said. Rex is a big fucking queen, is he alive? He did more than talk to the animals, my God, is Rex the dinosaur dead? I said…he was a fucking cute actor, talk to the fucking animals…

MADGE

Cut it Stuart, I loved that movie.

PROFESSOR
(*Singing*)
You want to talk to the animals, fuck all the animals…

MADGE
Cut it…

PROFESSOR
That's the way Rex sang it to me, BABE, NICE UNDERWATER SWIMMING, fuck all the animals, eat all the animals, milk all the animals, kill all the animals, outsmart all the animals…and get your money from all the animals, and buy your whoring street kids like animals, fuck all the animals, screw all the animals, screw all the screwables, buy all the animals, shoot all the animals…

MADGE
Cut it Stuart, you never knew Rex Harrison.

PROFESSOR
My dear Madge, have we had fun, up till now? Rex and I were so drunk one night that we got into this slapping fag fight. You don't even know what I'm talking about, and he kept the singing up, fuck all the animals, till I was laughing so hard that my stomach was ripping and he got me over on my knees. I was fucking twenty or nineteen and…

MADGE
Don't you dare. I loved Dr. Dolittle.

PROFESSOR
Doctor fucking screw me up the ass, Dolittle. Not pretty. Having fun my sweet, sexy Madge? Watch all the animals, screw all the animals…

MADGE
Yes, scary, horror fun, yes. You embarrass me. You really do.

PROFESSOR
Do you like Mexico? My sweet, hot Rego Park babe?

MADGE
I don't know.
(*Pause*)
You know what I wish? I wish we could go back to California, and

MADGE, continued
you could go back to being a movie star, and I wish my husband could see me on TV at the Academy Awards and made up and gorgeous and they call you up and you hold my hand and, and bring me up with you, and you say, "This woman, without this woman, I would have been a drunken number painter, so I want to thank this woman…to accept this award for me…Madge Roberts, my savior…

PROFESSOR
(*As if at the Academy Awards*)
…This woman who has made me realize, that Hollywood, and the shit it turns out, is an embarrassment to the human race and my great hope is that all the shit will get destroyed and never go into a child's mind, in a most natural disaster and a great siege on man and womankind and filmkind, and the insects again live and feed on the rotting brains of humans, directors and cheap screenwriters, and the explosives, that blow the minds of kids, and the shitty, reviewers that pay attention to crap, GO HIGHER BABE, and the beautiful crawling things that fill, and for good reason, my morning fear, JUMP BABE, JUST FUCKING JUMP. Look at that, Madge please, please stick with me, DIVE BABY. LOOK. BABE, YOU ARE BEAUTIFUL. LOOK AT HIS BODY, so fucking tough, he's gonna split the fucking moon, come on baby, let's make it shimmer. Look at him, kill the fucking bull, Madge, look, there's a fucking bull, right behind him, they are going to dive together. GO FUCKING BABE, GO.

MADGE
He's gonna die. There's no bull. I don't see a bull.

PROFESSOR
Look at him, gimme a fucking drink. The smoke from his nostrils, the huge cock pushing up his ass. SLAM HIM BABE. FUCKING SLAM HIM. Look at that, look at that, the bull is down, he's tough. BABE SLAM HIM, here it comes, the dive. LOOK AT THAT. WILL YOU LOOK AT THAT FUCKING SPLASH DOWN.

MADGE
Why are you so cruel, so mean, why do you enjoy your friends dying, splitting themselves from such heights. Why, Stuart?

PROFESSOR

Look at my bones with your x-ray machine, and the joints, look baby, look with open eyes and heart. Do you see the calcium, the fucking memories, the fucking dreams with their crab claws, open, hanging?

MADGE

You are so attractive, that's your game. Attractive, sadistic Stuart. The actor. You and your game are killing everything.

PROFESSOR

I have no game.

MADGE

You're full of fucking games, you sucked me into your game.

BABE
(*Yelling*)

I'm the champ, the champ, the champ of Mexico, the best, am I the best. I fuckin' survive. You're next, professor. You dive. You and your Madge.

PROFESSOR

You're the champion of men, Babe. I ascend the heights, alone, in darkness.

MADGE

I'll go with you. I'll dive and drown with you when you're sober, in the sunlight.

PROFESSOR

Madge, it's me and the luminescent jellyfish. I will do a swan dive into hell. The warm Pacific waters of hell. There is no love like true love. GO ALLEY, FUCKING DIVE. YOU DIVE, BABY. I'VE HIT THE BOTTOM, the fucking coral…

MADGE

Let's go back, think of it, interesting parts, you're a great man. My God, he can't dive from up there, My God, he must have been climbing all night. He's naked, even I can see that.

PROFESSOR

DIVE BABY, DIVE. Give me the fucking tequila. Look at him. Look at that from heaven, his liver, it will be poison fish food, all over the sea. ALLEY YOU ARE A FUCKING DIVER. A HIGH FUCKING DIVER, ALLEY, EAT SHIT, PUNK ASSHOLE. He's gonna take the Mexican babe with him, you see, they don't give a shit, they kiss, they are naked, up there on the dream, look at their sex on the cliff, how she bends, ALLEY YOU FUCKING BUM, DIVE BABY, DIVE. We're next, we are next. Are you coming, baby, are you coming? Hollywood is a bad idea, feel the warmth of your alive skin, the moon warmth, let's fucking die in the fall into the sea. Come on baby, be brave. Do you want to die an old woman, fucking ranting and raving? See how they hit the sea water, see the fucking luminescent, ancient jellyfish, think of the beauty of the splash. The hit, dividing the moon glitter. Get up baby, we dive.

MADGE

My kids. I am a mother, mother, mother you bastard, suicidal drunken bastard.

PROFESSOR

Fine, you watch the moon sink alone, I am going to dive, off the fucking cliff into the sea.

MADGE

Make love to me first, come on. Come on baby, then decide. No, in the sand – I call the shots. In the sand like the crabs.

PROFESSOR

My dear Madge, many years ago…

MADGE

I call the shots.

PROFESSOR

Stop it…

MADGE

Were you going to make love to me on the way down? The crash?

PROFESSOR

In every way. All over you.

MADGE

And you haven't missed out.

PROFESSOR

We fall into the sea, filled with life, fuck getting old. Have some tequila baby, enjoy. Look at that invitation, the fucking waves.

MADGE

Who am I? Do you know my name?

PROFESSOR

Midge or Madge or Mary, I don't, okay. I don't fucking know. God has only one name, one name, one fucking name. We climb the cliff and then we splash down, okay, okay, we slap into the sea, in the fucking moonlight. Madge, Midge, Mary you are a woman filled with fear and tears and heartfelt love, so fuck you. I am alone, always alone. Always the last one. Johnson dies, Alley dies, Sammy dies, BABE FLY, BABY. FLY YOU FIGHTER, FLY, BABE FLY OFF THE ROPES INTO HEAVEN.

MADGE

Do you know me? You are going to know me. You will know what is going on. You're not like them. You're better.

PROFESSOR

Better, no Madge, no better. Shall we my darling, trip the light fantastic, trust my dear, we will fly upward into the stars, the cosmos. Bam, bam, bam.

THOMAS
(*Appearing from the darkness*)

Madge?

MADGE

My God, Thomas.

THOMAS

It's me. Thank God I've found you. The children?

MADGE

Here.

THOMAS

Tucked in?

MADGE

Tucked in and safe. Thomas, this is Stuart.

PROFESSOR

Thomas old chap, you've made it. How terribly wonderful to meet you. Here, have as you chaps say, a hit, a shooter. You see, we've been having a bit of a diving exhibition.

THOMAS

Really?

MADGE

I'm so sorry Thomas.

THOMAS

I was on the diving team at Harvard.

PROFESSOR

Fantastic.

MADGE

My God, Thomas. I couldn't help myself.

PROFESSOR

DIVE YOU BASTARD, DIVE! Thomas, do you see the bull up there? Straight from the arena, he killed the matador and the picadors and all the horses, he killed the announcer and trumpeters. He broke

PROFESSOR, continued
through the walls of the arena. See the blood and wood on his horns? How majestically he stands on the cliff. Steam from the nostrils, his huge bull cock like a swinging pendulum designing the mandalas of the cosmos.

THOMAS
I don't see him, no. Stuart is it, Stuart?

PROFESSOR
Concentrate Thomas. He is fucking up there. He is about to dive in to the mandalas of the cosmos.

MADGE
You came all this way to find us?

PROFESSOR
He's going to dive. How many tons, Madge darling, how many tons do you think that creature weighs? MADGE, HOW MANY TONS? AND WILL HE FLY? Look at him go, that's something. Thomas did you see that? Did you see him fly? Giant bull, filled with tendencies. LOOK AT HIM. FUCKING TENDENCIES, ALL FLYING. And he goes up, up he bloody goes. A creature from some Thanksgiving Day parade.

THOMAS
The children are okay?

MADGE
Okay. It's been a learning experience.

THOMAS
Spanish as a second language…Madge, do they speak Spanish, a second language?

PROFESSOR
Did you see him? Did you see him oppose gravity, the bull in the ozone? My God, wake up, wake up. Madge, Thomas, you fuckers, did you see that?

THOMAS
I'm so glad I found you.

MADGE
Mexico, can you believe it, Mexico. Things could be different. I mean with us.

THOMAS
I haven't had dinner. I haven't had any dinner. Is there a restaurant around here? I've traveled a long way. Where can I get dinner?

MADGE
I don't know.

PROFESSOR
We must dive together, like the brave bulls. Thomas, my friend, the brave bulls as Hemingway once whispered in my ear as we made that terrible film, "Fuck them where they breathe". Thomas, do you comprehend the humor in that? Thomas old man, Hemingway and I in Cuba, fuck them where they breathe. That was his original title.

THOMAS
Let's get away from this man and discuss our…

MADGE
Our future, OUR FUTURE.

PROFESSOR
Kill him Madge. He's becoming a pain in the fucking ass, a real pain. Here, as Ernest said as the shark had his teeth around our Bluefish, fucking shoot him.

THOMAS
You can't. You bitch. You couldn't. You left me. I gave you everything.

MADGE
What did you call me? SAY IT.

THOMAS
The children are okay?

MADGE
What did you call me? The children are fine. SAY IT!

THOMAS
It slipped. After all this time, oh Madge, this loneliness, you are a mean bitch driven by sex. I am in so much pain, losing you to gangster bums.

MADGE
The words.

PROFESSOR
Shoot him darling, and get it over with. Look at that. Thomas, you will come back in the next, or next to life, a better person. Shoot him in his frontal lobe, where he keeps the policies.

THOMAS
I knew it. Right from the beginning, you never loved me. Nice house, nice car, you figured all along, this is a nice time, a nice life. I spent lots of money finding you. You won't get a cent. The Volvo, the Montessori school and now this bum, this English bum, drunk. I'll go dive. I'm done Madge. I loved you so much. I, I, I adore you.

MADGE
Sorry, Thomas.
(*Shoots him. PAUSE*)

PROFESSOR
Did you notice Madge, how more and more interesting you are becoming? I mean, physically more sexy. I mean your eyes, your breasts, your mouth, the way you move, talk to the animals. Touch all the animals, eat all the animals, fuck all the animals.

MADGE
Really. So we go back.

PROFESSOR

After the dive.

MADGE

If we survive we go to Hollywood.

PROFESSOR

We could float up, skyward.

MADGE

No more killing.

PROFESSOR

No more killing, just acting.

MADGE

No more drinking.

PROFESSOR

That would be impossible.

MADGE

Why?

PROFESSOR

Let's dive. The confusion, the diffusion of the brain…the, small personal parties, the daily celebration. I would miss the terror, the loneliness.

MADGE

Please…

PROFESSOR

I'll paint numbers all over you. Even numbers, odd numbers. GET AWAY FROM ME. Get away from the corpse, float you fucker, into the night, ALL OF YOU.

(*Pause*)

Look at the angel on the cliff, skyward pile up, one congested morning bridge to nowhere. The angel has a mustache not unlike my father's and breasts, or as you fucking Americans say, tits. Is that the right pronunciation, tits? Wings, look Madge, will you fucking wake

PROFESSOR, continued
up? Stand up. We are not in America, or Britain, fucking Mexico. I will never go back to Hollywood, or New York and the cheap shit they sell. Give me your lips Madge, arms, arms. We dive, we dive into the coral, the salt. Be brave, my love. I promise it will be okay.

MADGE
You promise, you promise.

PROFESSOR
Come on, my sweet. We dive, back arched, toes relaxed. The cliffs.

MADGE
In the sand, like the shellfish we are.

(*Fade MUSIC UP*)

Scene 3
SETTING: Movie set
AT RISE: DIRECTOR, STUART, MADGE

DIRECTOR
Now Stuart, the idea of this scene is desperation. Harold is upset at the idea of losing his wife. It's very tight and close up. Stuart, do you see your mark? Don't leave the shot. Watch your mark. Ready…Action!

STUART
"My darling, you are my life, my blood, my reality. Please don't leave me. How very much I love you. I will always love you, till time ends."

DIRECTOR
CUT, that is wonderful, brilliant, Stuart. Stuart, how nice to work with you again. So glad you're well, over your problem.

STUART
Thank you sir, nice to be back.

DIRECTOR
LUNCH! How was your vacation, New York, was it?

STUART
New York, Queens and a bit of Mexico, the beach you know.

DIRECTOR
With friends.

STUART
Close friends, from Freeport, Long Island. Cocktails and a bit of golf, some tennis, and a bit of diving, high diving – the cliffs you know, viewing creatures off the Mexican coast… the high dive, most exhilarating.

DIRECTOR
These vacations seem to give you even more added depth. Your talent has no limits, nice to have you on board Stuart. I wanted you for this film. The producers were against it, please don't prove me wrong. I've got a lot of money at stake. Can you handle a martini, I mean for lunch?

STUART
I think so. Thank you, Steven. Nice to be on board. Wonderful to be back in Hollywood.

DIRECTOR
Have some shrimp salad, really fresh.

MADGE
(*In a whisper*)
Stuart!

STUART
Oh, Steven , this is Midge.

MADGE
Madge.

STUART
This is Madge, Steven Spielberg, Madge.

DIRECTOR
Nice to meet you, excuse me. Oh and Stuart, I know how much you object to violence and gratuitous sex in films, but it sells tickets. These are the nineties. What can I say?...Thank you Stuart.

STUART
I understand Steven.

DIRECTOR
You won't be sorry, my dear friend Stuart. Jesus. Amazing. I mean it. Take care Midge.

MADGE
MADGE! What is the problem? MADGE!
(*Pause*)
Stuart, that was wonderful. The scene, it was wonderful.

STUART
God forgive me.

(*Picks up bottle and looks at the sky*)

(*MUSIC UP*)
END OF PLAY

Don and Tom

Don and Tom 2003

First Production, Pearl's
Burlington, VT
Directed by the Author

Original Cast

Tom – Paul Soychak
Don – Aaron Masi
Dr. – Al Salzman
Dad – John Alexander
Mom – Dawn Kearon
Girl (G) – Alissa Juvan
Priest – John Alexander

Cast of Characters

Tom – A small man
Don – A tall, frightening man
Dr. – A shrink.
Dad (Sal) – Tom's father
Mom – Tom's mother
Girl (G) – A young woman
Priest – a Priest

Don and Tom

(Half dark stage
Smashing and crashing sounds
Tommy's kneeling, banging on the floor.)

TOM
No...No...No...No...Stop...Stop...Stop...Please...Stop...

BLACK OUT-SILENCE

TOM
No...No...No...No...Stop...Stop...Stop...Please...

BLACK OUT-SILENCE

TOM
Stop it...Stop it...Stop it...(faster) Stop it...Stop it...Stop it...Stop it.

BLACK OUT-SILENCE

(Mom appears stage left and crosses to downstage right and exits.)

BLACK OUT – CRASHING SOUNDS UP

TOM
Don't you talk to my mother, don't you touch my mother, get away from my mother. Stop it!

BLACK OUT-SOFT HUM

TOM
Mommy...mommy...mommy...mommy...mommy.

DAD

Shut Up!

TOM

Mommy...mommy...mommy...mommy...mommy.

DAD

Shut it!

MOM

Leave him alone!

DAD

Shut up! You bitch, you lousy bitch, lousy stinking bitch.

(DAD smashes MOM.)
BLACK OUT

TOM
(Doing a little soft shoe and singing)

You are my sunshine, my only shoe shine. You make me happy when shoes are gray.

MOM

Honey, walk the dog, wash the car, clean the toilet, put the clothes in the dryer, mow the lawn, do the dishes, get me a drink, with a mixer and ice... then go to the store and get some...did you forget the ironing?

DAD

Do you know what you are? Well? Well? Well?

MOM

Leave him alone.

TOM

Don't leave me alone, please not alone in the dark, the hall light, don't shut it off, don't, please not the dark.

BLACK OUT
SILENCE

(*A DOCTOR is interviewing TOM.*)

TOM
My mother's name is Anna and she comes from Antarctica and she loves apples. My father's name is Arnie he comes from Abalone and he loves Absoluteness.

DR.
What is that suppose to mean?

TOM
My dog's name is Atom Bomb he comes from anagram and he loves arms. I'm not good.

DR.
Not good? What gives you the right to be good? No one is good.

TOM
I'm…Avoid I come from Accident and I love anti…anti…anti…anti ants…(*laughing hard*) Anti antdom.

DR.
Stop it! What are you…

TOM
Con…

DR.
Confused.

TOM
Worse.

DR.
Worse? Who is the President of the United States of America?

TOM
I don't know.

DR.
What year is it?

TOM
I don't know.

DR.
How long have you been here?

TOM
Too long, two long johns, one dirty one clean.

DR.
Are you better or worse?

TOM
Much worse, like…

DR.
Like…

TOM
Lake.

DR.
Like…

TOM
Lake, a lake front, we had a lake front, a house on the lake. My name is Billy, I come from Bigtown and I love Bagel Blossoms. My name is…

DR.
Stop it! Shut it! Thank you. Now according to my report…

TOM
What report?

DR.
Right here, the report, it says here, Mr. Downs, you lived in a third floor, slum, tenement, one room apartment…

TOM
That's wrong, completely wrong.

DR.
If you continue to lie, I'll have to take measures.

TOM
What measures?

DR.
Incarceration for life, in the prison for the criminally insane, or execution.

TOM
My name is Tommy, I lived in a tenement and I love . ten…ten…ten…tinnitus. Don't you mean hospital?

DR.
Listen to me Mr. Downs, don't you ever, ever, correct me, do you understand?

TOM
Yes, I'm sorry, I didn't mean to…

DR.
Did you mean to murder your parents?

TOM
What? Pinkerton and I love our parents.

DR.
Don't you ever make me repeat myself, I'm an extremely busy man. Did you mean to kill your parents?

                    TOM
Doctor Pinkerton, I love my parents.

                    DR.
And did they love you?

                    TOM
Yes Doctor Pinkerton, they do love me.

                    DR.
Did love you.

                    TOM
Do love me.

                    DR.
Did love you.

                    TOM
Do love me.

                    DR.
Did love you.

                    TOM
Do love me.

                    DR.
STOP IT! Did, you are mixing up tenses Mr. Downs, get that through your head, did, did, did. They're dead Tommy, you're parents are dead as door stops…

                    TOM
Tommy? My name is Alfie I come from Amishtown and I eat Anchovies…

                    DR.
GET HIM OUT OF HERE! NOW!

                    BLACK OUT

TOM

We had a lake house we'd go to in the summer, up in Maine, me, mom and dad and Buster, our Collie. Boy did I love that place. Me and Dad would go fishing in our little boat, it had one of those silent trolling motors, I called the motor Pelli, because it looked like a black Pelican. And, oh boy, did we catch fish, speckled trout, perch, it would sort of freak me out to see them gasping for air, or water, whatever they were gasping for, it seemed like a terrible death, but dad would say, "Son, they are only fish". We'd bring them back, hanging from a piece of fishing line with a stick tied to each end, in the gills out the mouth, in the gills out the mouth. It was my job to clean them, on a box in the backyard, cut out their hearts and guts, cut off their heads, sometimes I'd see the stuff in their stomachs, smaller fish, only fish to the bigger fish. I'd put the heads and guts in a bucket, boy did the flies love that stuff, I had a fly swatter, bam, bam, bam, they're only flies. Mom would fry them up in butter, only fish. We'd have them with mom's potato salad. Boy that was great, till I got a fishbone stuck in my throat, mom made me eat bread, dad laughed so hard the beer came out of his nose. I think I lost consciousness, choking and all, it was hard to swallow for weeks, mom finally took me to the doctor. I still have this scar on my throat where they made the incision.

BLACK OUT

PRISON CELL

DON

I just got here, but I know why you're here.

TOM

Really?

DON

Word has it, you killed your parents, twenty years ago? Is that right? That's nice, so cool, that takes balls, good for you. Runny Jello? Hey Tommy, you ever snort raw Jello powder? You better fuckin' answer me or I'll snap your little neck. Did you ever snort raw Jello powder?

TOM

Yes. Okay, yes.

DON

You see we're a team. I did Strawberry and Banana-Strawberry… What a rush. You know why I'm here?

TOM

Leave me alone.

DON

I'll tell you why, between you and me. They say I raped a little girl, that's pretty fucked up, isn't it? (*Pause*) They say I killed her afterwards, after I raped her. (*Pause*) You know what's fucked up? Hey Tommy! Tommy! Sorry, sorry to yell. Tommy? Respond buddie.

TOM

Yeah.

DON

We're roommates, buddie, buddies. Don and Tom, that's pretty good isn't it. Isn't it! Don and Tom. You get it, don't you? Don and Tom. None of this "E" shit. No Tommy-Donny shit, we're not babies.

TOM

Yeah, Don and Tom, Don and Tom, Don and Tom, (*Laughing*) Donny and Tommy (*Laughing out of control*)…

DON

Okay! Do you know what's fucked up? (*Pause*) Well I'll tell you. What's fucked up is that they have a word for it. Having sex with someone against their will. Rape. Now I think the word, rape, came before it ever happened. You know what I think?

TOM

No. Stop it, (*laughing*) okay? Leave me alone, okay? (*Laughing*)

DON

It's not fuckin' funny, I'll snap your fuckin' neck, now shut it!

TOM

You're funny man, here snap me! Go, go, go.

DON
Now listen, I think there were a bunch of perverts sitting in a dark room, around a table, thinking up words and one guy says; What if a guy grabs someone and does them against their will, you know what I mean by, does them? Has unwanted sex, that's what that means. So the guy says, what do we call that? They think about that stuff. How do they come up with rape? The word, rape. What do you think? Tommy? We're roommates Tommy. How do they come up with that word? Rape.

TOM
I don't know, I can't think about it. Okay, okay, I don't know.

DON
Now listen. I figure they are rich guys, I mean inventing words and shit, the word inventors, around a big oak table, do you see that? Like they have scrabble pieces but they're made of gold and silver, no board or those stupid trays, just letters. Anyway, they have a big bowl of red seedless grapes on the table, you know something to munch on while they're inventing words, a guy thinks grape and says rape, like he's tired and doesn't articulate the G, rape, so they can move on. What do you think? Like, me, I see this word invention shit happening. Do you see that Tom? I think about this shit. Grapes, Rapes. Like in your case; Murder, hurt her. You get it? Murder, hurt her. So Tom, how'd you do it? Knife, gun, you look like a suffocation guy. Tom, that's a compliment. How'd you do it? Black garbage bags over mommy and daddy's head, let them try to breathe? Was that it?

TOM
I love my family. Your name is Don you come from downtown and you love donut dough dreams.

DON
Don-Tom. Yeah, I thought that at first, bad dream, I would never hurt a fly, I could not kill a fly. You know what they did? Do you know what they did? They showed me these terrible photographs, of a little dead girl. They are gonna do this to you Tommy, so pay attention, I can't believe it, they made me dig her up, that's pretty bad, right, Tom? Hey Tommy, you answer to Tommy, right? Help me, okay, we

DON. continued

can help each other, you know, like both in the same boat kind of thing. We can be friends, you know, like buddies, Tommy? We can. Twenty years, one day, same deal. When every day is the same, no more time. Hey Tom, you want a blow job?

BLACK OUT

TOM
(to audience)

At the lake house, down the beach, there were these two sisters, Laurie and Glorie, Laurie was 12, Glorie was 14, same age as me, we used to swim together, in June the lake was freezing, we would jump in and jump out, then huddle under a big beach towel, oh boy that felt good, they would pull down my bathing suit and my heart would pound, Glorie would pull her top down, her breasts were the most beautiful things I ever saw, then Laurie would kiss me on the lips, her mouth had this popcorn taste, it was the best, the best, it was the first, my heart almost jumped through my chest.

BLACK OUT

FAMILY KITCHEN

WOMAN

You know Sal, you drink too much beer, it makes you ugly.

DAD

Yeah, well why don't you learn to cook. Boiled hot dogs? Tommy, get the ketchup. Get it! This fuckin' kid is an idiot. Get the ketchup, jerk-off idiot.

TOM

I'm going, I'm getting ketchup.

MOM

Sal, try to control yourself, he's a human being.

DAD

He's a fuckin' idiot freak. You gave birth to a freak. He plays with himself in bed. Don't you, idiot, idiot boy.

MOM

He tries, give him a break.

DAD

I pay money for his food, his bed, his clothes, he's not my son, look at him, not mine, he is not mine.

MOM

Don't start this. You know damn well he's your son, our son Tommy.

DAD

Who did you screw to get him, who goddam it, who, what deformed idiot? What deformed idiot that would put it to you?

MOM

He is your son, now cut it!

DAD

No, he's not my kid. Look at him, look at him. He doesn't have my bones, jerk-off idiot.
(*He grabs Tommy by the neck.*)

TOM

Mom, mom.

MOM

Leave him alone.

DAD

Oh I'll leave him alone all right, I'll leave you both alone.

TOM

Dad, let go, that hurts…

DAD

Don't you call me dad, don't you ever call me that again, do you understand, do you?

TOM
Yes.

DAD
Sir, you call me sir. Now get out of my sight. Go! You make me sick, like your mother's cooking. Sickening.

BLACK OUT

GIRL (G)
(to audience)
He was a nice guy, we met at high school, freshman year, you know, he was quiet, he tried to ask me out, but he put it in a funny way, he couldn't really ask me, we went to the movies once, I didn't like him touching me. All he did was try to put his arm around me, his hands were all clammy, no. I didn't like that, I mean his hands, and his body had this funny smell, like, like bleach, like when my mother did the white wash, bleach, yeah that was his smell, bleach. So after the movie, that scary one with Jack Nicholson, he just walked away from me, I mean he didn't ever walk me home, I walked home alone, he just sort of disappeared, no goodbye, nothing. I was glad to get rid of him.

TOM
My first date with G was the best, we saw, what was it, the one where there is all this dancing, yeah, yeah, a musical, really romantic. When I put my arm around her she got all hot, we had this tender kiss, God, her lips were so soft. I wanted to marry her right then and there. I could tell she liked me. She liked me a lot. After I walked her home, I called her, we talked all night.

GIRL (G)
He scared me, I knew he was in trouble, but that Sunday morning I was in church, and the priest gave this sermon about being understanding to people, so I went to the movie with him. The phone rang at about 5AM. I picked it up so not to wake my parents, I kept it off the hook till I got up for school. He was waiting outside as I was leaving for school, he looked like he didn't sleep, I told him I wanted to walk alone.

TOM
I stayed up all night, we talked on the phone all night. I picked some flowers on the way to her house in the morning. I walked her to school. I could tell she loved me. She was crazy about me. We had a thing, me and G, we had a great thing.

BLACK OUT

CELL

DON
Tom, do you know what was going through my mind when I did it? Tom? I'll never tell them I did it, but I did. I thought it was clean, with a child, it was clean. It was bad, I knew that after it started, there was no going back. It's bad what I did, innocent, till she…Tom, I like the meds, I feel okay. You? Tom? You and me, we could break out of here, partners. I figure we could become airline pilots, little private jets. Get a little jet company, Don and Tom Jets. Little fighter planes, up in the sky, screaming around the sky. People would pay a lot of money for that. Take them any place they wanted to go, see, movies stars would be our best customers. Do you see that? Me and you with radio contact. Hello Tom, it's Don, I got Hillary Clinton up here, Over. I said over…Tom fucking answer, over…Who do you have? Tom, you there? Who do you have?

TOM
The President, George Bush.

DON
There you go, we're screaming through the clouds. I'm takin Hillary to Uganda. Tom, where you takin George?

TOM
The moon, Don, the moon.

DON
Tom?

TOM
Yeah.

                    DON
You want a blow job?

                    TOM
I'm okay.

                    DON
Tom.

                    TOM
Yeah?

                    DON
Will you give me one, I'm hurtin' pal. I got court tomorrow.

                    TOM
I'm okay.

                    DON
I'm scared they won't renew my pilot's license. I need to fly. Help me out, one night.

                    TOM
Don. I can't, I just can't.

                    DON
I understand, it's okay.

Sound of Planes

BLACK OUT

CELL

                    PRIEST
Do you understand what you did?

                    DON
No sir.

PRIEST

You?

TOM

What?

PRIEST

Tell me what you did.

TOM

I can't.

PRIEST

I said, tell me what you did.

DON

He said he can't.

PRIEST

You shut up!

TOM

Leave Don alone.

PRIEST

You men better talk to me.

DON

Why is that?

PRIEST

I'm your only hope.

TOM

I don't want any hope.

DON

Me neither.

TOM

Me neither.

PRIEST

You want God to forgive you?

DON

No.

TOM

Me neither.

PRIEST

You men want to spend eternity in hell? Mr. Downs?

TOM

Yes.

DON

So do I.

PRIEST

All you have to do is admit your crimes and ask God for forgiveness.

TOM

I didn't do anything.

DON

Me neither.

PRIEST

Jesus is in this room, do you understand that?

DON

I didn't do anything.

PRIEST

You raped a little girl.

                                DON

I don't think so.

                                TOM

He…he…doesn't think so.

                                DON

I didn't do anything.

                               PRIEST

All you have to do is admit your crimes, your sins, and ask for forgiveness. Then you'll be spared eternal damnation. Now come on men, let's get down on our knees and get this over with.

                                TOM

On our knees? I don't get it.

                                DON

Me neither.

                                TOM

Me neither.

                               PRIEST

You men understand, you are both going to be executed, lethal injections, or in this state is it the hot seat? No injections it is. Like dogs, you men will be put to death like dogs, or do they gas dogs? Do you men know?

                                TOM

I don't know.

                                DON

Me neither.

                                TOM

My dog Buster was run over by a milk truck.

DON
My dog Charlie fell out the window.

TOM
My parakeet Freddy got stuck in a plastic garbage bag.

DON
My cat Frisky fell into the washing machine; hot wash, rinse and spin, rinse and spin.

TOM
My turtle Bangie feel down the basement stairs.

PRIEST
That's all very sad and unfortunate but, it doesn't give you the right to rape and murder. Now goddamit let's get down on our knees and ask the Lord in heaven for forgiveness, I don't have all day. (*The men stand there*) Hey look! I dropped my cigarettes. (*The men kneel to pick them up*) Do you ask the Lord in heaven for forgiveness and do you want to keep my cigarettes?

TOM
Yeah.

DON
Me too.

PRIEST
Okay, up you go. Jesus, that took forever.

TOM
My knees hurt.

DON
Mine too.

TOM
I feel dizzy.

                    DON

Me too.

                    PRIEST

You men got up too fast. Take deep breaths, like this.

                    DON

I don't want to.

                    TOM

Me neither.

                    PRIEST

I'll see you at the execution.

                    (*Exit*)

                    DON

Man, I'm really dizzy.

                    TOM

Me too. Whoooo.

                    DON

Tom? You know what he did, he tricked us. Tom?

                    TOM

Yeah?

                    DON

You want my cigarettes? I don't smoke.

                    TOM

Me neither.

                    DON

Tom, listen, we need a plan, I'm not ready to die. Tom, for me you've got to fight the medication. Fucking mind control. Say it Tom: mind control, come on, mind control. Fuckin' say it!

TOM
Mind control. Fuckin' Mind Control!

DON
We're drugged, little pills down the stomach, into the digestive wall, into the blood and into the brain.

TOM
It's not that simple.

DON
Yeah but we're talking, we can think, not real lucid, I'm not that lucid, but I can think, not so lucid. Tom?

TOM
Yeah, not so lucid. I tried to hide the pills under my tongue, in my cheek.

DON
I swallow the shit, then I tell my stomach wall: No fuckin' entry, keep out of my brain.

TOM
You said, you said before, you said you like the meds.

DON
I control them, Tom and you can too. Like a cocktail, a sip here and there. Come in, keep out. Control over the stomach lining. I'm gonna ask you a simple question, I want this question, these words, to enter the free part of your brain. I'm not fuckin' around. Do you want to get out of here? Don't answer right away; let it go to the part that has freedom. Do you want to get out of here?

TOM
They are going to kill us, aren't they?

DON
That's good pal, you're waking up. Keep your brain in that place. Mind Control.

TOM
I want to go back to the lake house with the girls.

DON
Now pay attention. We are going to erase our crimes, for good and forever. Tom , I'm going to touch your head, is that okay with you?

TOM
I'm afraid, I don't know.

DON
I am the fucking King Kong healer, I have healing magnets in my fingers. I'll clear you Tom, you have to say it's okay.

TOM
I'm afraid.

DON
No man, fear is what they thrive on, I'll clear you Tom, then we leave this shit hole.

TOM
Why me, why now?

DON
Tom, we leave this shit hole, for now and forever. You are the only one here and I can't do it alone.

TOM
Alone, alone, you're fuckin' stupid, Don, you don't get it, alone is all there is. I don't even like you, I hate your voice, your sound, your smell, your fuckin' bag of skin.

DON
Now you listen to me, I know how to get out of here. But I've got to demagnetize your brain. Then you demagnetize me.

(*Chases Tom around.*)

TOM

No man, no, please no. Guard! Guard!

DON

Okay, okay, Tom. Calm down buddie, it's okay. Look, I want to show you something, (*he takes out a red handkerchief*) Look Tom, it takes two to tango. (*He swings it around*) Mind control, buddy.

TOM

Let me see that.

DON

No way.

TOM

It's nice, Don, let me touch it. Don, come on.

DON

Okay Tom, we make a simple trade. You can have it. Wait! Don't grab. Will you let me demagnetize you?

TOM

Damn it, you mean that's the deal?

DON

That's the deal.

TOM

Okay, but I'm scared.

DON

I know buddie, now let's do it.

(*They slowly exchange the cloth, Don touches Tom's head. Tom touches Don's head and tears the handkerchief in half. They tie each half around their heads. They sit like they're in their planes. Sound of jets taking off.*)

DON
Don calling Tom, Don calling Tom. Over.

TOM
Yeah Don, I'm up there , it's beautiful. Over.

DON
Who do you have? Over.

TOM
George Bush. You?

(*The Priest Appears, slowly gives them injections. They ignore him.*)

PRIEST
This is it, men. God forgives you for your sins.

DON
You got to say, "Over".

TOM
Over.

DON
I got Hillary Clinton, she's hot, Tom.

TOM
Hey Don, can I trade, George for Madonna? Oh yeah, Over.

DON
It's done. Over.

TOM
She's hot Don, she's sitting on my lap. Over.

DON
Do her Tom, do her, just watch where you're going.

TOM
I can't, her beautiful blond hair is in my eyes. Over.

DON
Autopilot Tom, put it on autopilot. Hillary's on me. Over and out.

TOM
Don, hey Don, don't fuck around, Don? Over and out.

(They both slump in their seats.)
Sound of jets

SLOW FADE
MUSIC UP: Sinatra "Fly Me to the Moon"

END OF PLAY

Fomite
Burlington, VT

A fomite is a medium capable of transmitting infectious organisms from one individual to another.

"The activity of art is based on the capacity of people to be infected by the feelings of others." Tolstoy, *What Is Art?*

Writing a review on Amazon, Good Reads, Shelfari, Library Thing or other social media sites for readers will help the progress of independent publishing. To submit a review, go to the book page on any of the sites and follow the links for reviews. Books from independent presses rely on reader to reader communications.

Visit http://www.fomitepress.com/FOMITE/Our_Books.html
for more information or to order any of our books.

As It Is On Earth
Peter M Wheelwright

Dons of Time
Greg Guma

Loisaida
Dan Chodorkoff

My Father's Keeper
Andrew Potok

My God, What Have We Done
Susan V Weiss

Rafi's World
Fred Russell

Fomite
Burlington, VT

The Co-Conspirator's Tale
Ron Jacobs

Short Order Frame Up
Ron Jacobs

All the Sinners Saints
Ron Jacobs

Travers' Inferno
L. E. Smith

The Consequence of Gesture
L. E. Smith

Raven or Crow
Joshua Amses

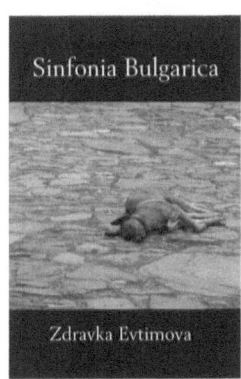

Sinfonia Bulgarica
Zdravka Evtimova

The Good Muslim
of Jackson Heights
Jaysinh Birjépatil

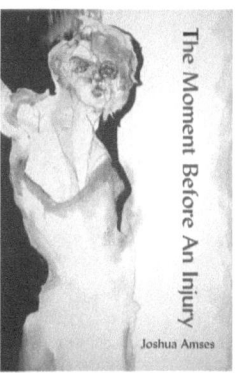

The Moment Before an Injury
Joshua Amses

Fomite
Burlington, VT

The Return of
Jason Green
Suzi Wizowaty

Victor Rand
David Brizeri

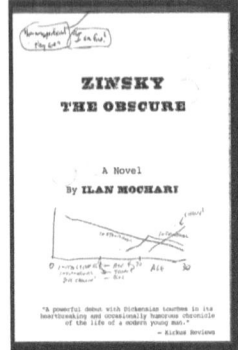

Zinsky the Obscure
Ilan Mochari

Body of Work
Andrei Guruianu

Carts and Other Stories
Zdravka Evtimova

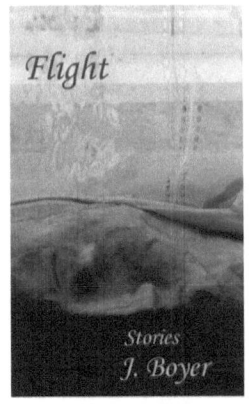

Flight
Jay Boyer

Love's Labours
Jack Pulaski

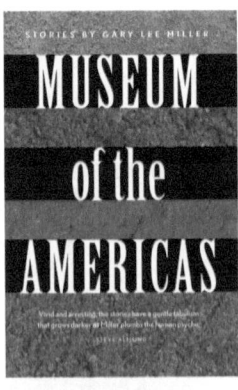

Museum of the Americas
Gary Lee Miller

Saturday Night at Magellan's
Charles Rafferty

Fomite
Burlington, VT

Signed Confessions
Tom Walker

Still Time
Michael Cocchiarale

Suite for Three Voices
Derek Furr

Unfinished Stories of Girls
Catherine Zobal Dent

Views Cost Extra
L. E. Smith

Visiting Hours
Jennifer Anne Moses

When You Remeber
Deir Yassin
R. L. Green

Alfabestiaro
Antonello Borra

Cycling in Plato's Cave
David Cavanagh

Fomite
Burlington, VT

AlphaBetaBestiario
Antonello Borra

Entanglements
Tony Magistrale

Everyone Lives Here
Sharon Webster

Four-Way Stop
Sherry Olson

Improvisational Arguments
Anna Faktorovitch

Loosestrife
Greg Delanty

Meanwell
Janice Miller Potter

Roadworthy Creature
Roadworth Craft
Kate Magill

The Derivation of
Cowboys & Indians
Joseph D. Reich

Fomite
Burlington, VT

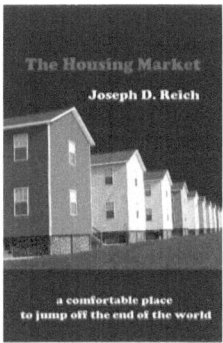

The Housing Market
Joseph D. Reich

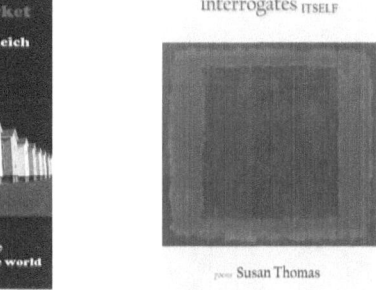

The Empty Notebook
Interrogates Itself
Susan Thomas

The Hundred Yard
Dash Man
Barry Goldensohn

The Listener Aspires
to the Condition of Music
Barry Goldensohn

The Way None
of This Happened
Mike Breiner

Screwed
Stephen Goldberg

Planet Kasper
Peter Schumann

My Murder
and Other Local News
David Schein

Picking Up the Bodies
James F. Connolly

www.ingramcontent.com/pod-product-compliance
Lightning Source LLC
Chambersburg PA
CBHW030307080526
44584CB00012B/474